THE LOVERS

THE HIGH PRIESTESS

THE HIEROPHANT

THE HERMIT

THE MAGICIAN

THE HANGED MAN

THE FOOL

THE EMPRESS

THE MOON

THE EMPEROR

THE CHARIOT

THE DEVIL

THE STAR

THE WORLD

THE TOWER

THE SUN

TAROT
THROUGH THE
WITCH'S YEAR

33 SPREADS FOR
SPIRITUAL
CONNECTION

KAREN KREBSER

Microcosm Publishing
Portland, Ore | Cleveland, Ohio

TAROT THROUGH THE WITCH'S YEAR: 33 SPREADS FOR SPIRITUAL CONNECTION

© Karen Krebser, 2024
© This edition Microcosm Publishing 2024
First edition – 3,000 copies – April 23, 2024
ISBN 9781648419874
This is Microcosm # 632
Cover by Lindsey Cleworth
Illustrated by Gerta O. Egy
Edited by Olivia Rollins

Design by Joe Biel

To join the ranks of high-class stores that feature Microcosm titles, talk to your rep:
In the U.S. **COMO** (Atlantic), **ABRAHAM** (Midwest), **BOB BARNETT** (Texas, Oklahoma, Arkansas, Louisiana), **IMPRINT** (Pacific), **TURNAROUND** (UK), **UTP/ MANDA** (Canada), **NEWSOUTH** (Australia/New Zealand), **Observatoire** (Africa, Middle East, Europe), **Yvonne Chau** (Southeast Asia), **HarperCollins** (India), **Everest/ B.K. Agency** (China), **Tim Burland** (Japan/Korea), and **FAIRE** and **EMERALD** in the gift trade.

For a catalog, write or visit:
Microcosm Publishing
2752 N Williams Ave.
Portland, OR 97227

All the news that's fit to print at www.Microcosm.Pub/Newsletter.

For a full-color version of all the Tarot spreads, we offer a discounted ebook at **Microcosm.Pub/TarotYear** with coupon code TAROTEBOOK.

Did you know that you can buy our books directly from us at sliding scale rates? Support a small, independent publisher and pay less than Amazon's price at **www. Microcosm.Pub.**

Global labor conditions are bad, and our roots in industrial Cleveland in the '70s and '80s made us appreciate the need to treat workers right. Therefore, our books are MADE IN THE USA.

Library of Congress Cataloging-in-Publication Data

Names: Krebser, Karen, author.
Title: Tarot through the witch's year : 33 spreads for spiritual connection / by Karen Krebser.
Description: Portland : Microcosm Publishing, [2024] | Summary: ""Explore the spiritual patterns of the Tarot with this collection of spreads based on the pagan Wheel of the Year. Reflecting earth-honoring spiritualities, Tarot Through the Witch's Year presents divination in a welcoming, inclusive, non-judgmental, and informative way. Readers, novice and proficient alike, are invited to dive headfirst into the spirituality involved in the witch's year and to approach divine energy as it moves us and the Great Wheel around. The thirty-three spreads include layouts, images, diagrams, and sample readings for the four equinoxes and solstices, the four cross-quarter days, thirteen full moons, and twelve dark moons. Readers in both the Northern and Southern Hemispheres will find valuable insight and tools as they navigate their year, beginning at any point on the calendar. See your year through new eyes, finding deeper meanings and a greater sense of connectedness""-- Provided by publisher.
Identifiers: LCCN 2023050628 | ISBN 9781648419874 (hardcover)
Subjects: LCSH: Tarot. | Sabbat.
Classification: LCC BF1879.T2 K75 2024 | DDC 133.3/2424--dc23/eng/20240226
LC record available at https://lccn.loc.gov/2023050628

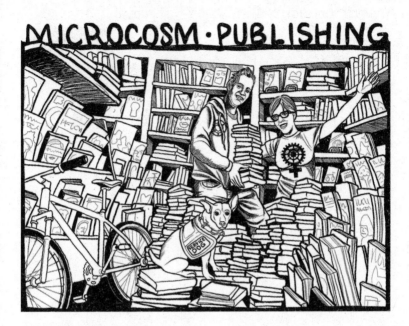

MICROCOSM PUBLISHING is Portland's most diversified publishing house and distributor, with a focus on the colorful, authentic, and empowering. Our books and zines have put your power in your hands since 1996, equipping readers to make positive changes in their lives and in the world around them. Microcosm emphasizes skill-building, showing hidden histories, and fostering creativity through challenging conventional publishing wisdom with books and bookettes about DIY skills, food, bicycling, gender, self-care, and social justice. What was once a distro and record label started by Joe Biel in a drafty bedroom was determined to be *Publishers Weekly*'s fastest-growing publisher of 2022 and #3 in 2023, and is now among the oldest independent publishing houses in Portland, OR, and Cleveland, OH. We are a politically moderate, centrist publisher in a world that has inched to the right for the past 80 years.

CONTENTS

Introduction

A young man stands on a lonely beach, the waves rolling in quietly and endlessly behind him, a light breeze pushing the waves ashore and ruffling the feathers in his fancy hat. His clothing is ornate, clean, unpatched, unstained, and his boots are slightly too big for him; it looks like he's wearing a uniform of some kind, declaring himself as a functionary of some local authority perhaps, a worker or a soldier for someone in charge. As he stands with his back to the sea, we begin to wonder what he's doing there. He holds a large ceremonial cup out in front of him, a chalice of some kind, and of all things there's a small fish popping out of the water it contains. We rub our eyes because it's hard to believe what we're seeing: it looks like the sparkling little fish is speaking to the young man, who listens intently. What messages are being conveyed by this denizen of the watery depths? What magical possibilities are opening up as wisdom is passed from one realm to another?

If you are at all familiar with the Tarot, you will already have recognized this description as one possible representation of the Page of Cups, a sweet and naïve youth who is all heart and feelings and is just beginning to explore the connections, imagery, and messages from the realm of the unseen, the unconscious, the magical realm of the heart that we all have access to. Depending on the question being asked, the Page of Cups could be speaking of being open to a new relationship, being too naïve in a relationship, or even dithering about whether direct action is called for. And depending on the focus of the reading—for example, whether the reading is exploring one's shadow or how best to develop practices to work on healing trauma, or even if fortune-telling is the object of the reading—the meanings of the card will shift.

We may be living through a golden age of divination right now. Tarot decks are commonplace purchases at many bookstores, and while a few people frown upon fortune-telling and see the cards as something evil, that point of view is about as far from my own as is the moon. The world around us is a mystery, and discovering answers to the mystery is my *raison d'être*. I might as well have been born with a Tarot deck in my hands, or a pair of dice, or the Norse runes; that's how often and how thoroughly I've always relied upon divination in my life to communicate with the mystery of the world around us. I was raised Catholic in the late '60s and early '70s, however, which meant that my family stayed far away from the occult, and it wasn't until my first trip to a Renaissance faire in the early 1990s that I found and purchased my first Tarot deck. I began to study it in earnest in the early 2000s, when I lived next door to a giant bookstore and was able to find all kinds of resources to teach me about the Tarot. Books by Mary K. Greer, Rachel Pollack, and Allyson Walsh led the way, but I found many books that deal with the divinatory aspects of the Tarot, the card meanings, and their history. They detail how this pack of 78 cards went from an artistic gift among kings and queens to a key for discussing the political and philosophical issues of the day to a parlor game (gamblers, rejoice!) to one of the most popular divination tools in Western history. I have many of these excellent books in my personal collection and have included several in the references section of this book for readers looking for resources. And an abundance of classes, workshops, conferences, and seminars have blossomed around the world since those days of living next to the bookstore. These teach the uses of the Tarot, as well as many other divination systems, and allow the seeker to explore an entire world of humanity's attempts to communicate with the ancestors, the gods, and the natural world.

This book will use the cards in a different way from the above, however. The structure of this book is based on the witch's Wheel of the Year (also called the Great Wheel), a construct deeply rooted in Irish pagan spirituality that is used throughout the Western world to connect with the seasons of the year and the movement of the sun and moon. This Wheel of the Year is actually a combination of two overlapping wheels: one that tracks the four great Irish fire festivals (Imbolg, Bealtaine, Lúnasa, and Samhain) and another that tracks the equinoxes and solstices as the sun moves through its annual orbit. There is a wonderful blog post, video, and class about this by Irish Draoí (the Irish word for "Druid") Lora O'Brien of the Irish Pagan School, who takes the time to explain how these two wheels move and thrive together within the living practice of Irish paganism.[1] A link to the Irish Pagan School is included in the reference section of this volume, and those who want to delve more deeply into the authentic Irish way of practicing pagan spirituality will find many terrific resources at that site, both paid-for and free. I mention this here, right up front, because it's important to give credit where credit is due, and credit is indeed due to the practitioners and keepers of the Irish pagan traditions who passed down their learning between the generations. As a supporter of the Irish Pagan School, I feel it's important that they be recognized and honored.

In this book we'll look at the different fire festivals and the fixed positions of the sun, when it seems to freeze as if on a tipping point prior to falling back into rhythm with daily sunrises and sunsets. We won't be looking only at earthly and heavenly fire in this book, though: we are also going to be paying close attention to our nearest astral neighbor, the moon, by tracking full moons and dark moons throughout the year.

Let me stop here and explain a little about what I mean when I say "dark moon." Many calendars include the phases of the moon and refer to the stage when the moon is covered in shadow as the "new moon." I'm choosing the phrase "dark moon" purposefully to refer to that time, however, because this term more accurately describes the period between when the old moon is completely

1 You can find Lora O'Brien's resources at loraobrien.ie/irish-pagan-holidays.

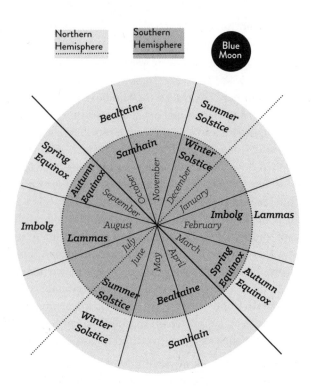

Northern Hemisphere

Southern Hemisphere

Blue Moon

Bealtaine

Summer Solstice

Spring Equinox

Samhain

Winter Solstice

Autumn Equinox

September

October

November

December

January

Imbolg

Lammas

Imbolg

February

August

Lammas

July

March

June

May

April

Spring Equinox

Autumn Equinox

Summer Solstice

Bealtaine

Winter Solstice

Samhain

A modified version of the witch's Wheel of the Year, around which this book is organized. The fire festivals and quarter days for both hemispheres are represented, as is the wild-card blue moon.

enshadowed and when the new moon emerges. A new moon is visible while a dark moon is not, and it's that time when the moon is hidden in shadow that we will be dealing with directly here. It provides us with an opportunity to "go dark," to go within, to go deep underground (metaphorically), to visit with and listen to our own shadow, to learn about how we are when faced with darkness—both as an absence of light and as a representation of what we hide from the world.

Full moons are generally regarded as times of expansion, of big thinking and big dreaming as a way to jump-start plans or processes or ideas. "Project time!" That could very well be the motto of any of our full moons throughout the year. Dark moons are the opposite: the time during the month when it is advised to retreat and draw inward to rest and recover from all that expansion. It's a time to consider, to reflect and review what went on during the expansive full-moon phase, and to begin incorporating lessons learned. Mother Nature has provided both cycles for us because She knows (even if we don't) that we need rest. We can't be going full-throttle all the time, no matter how much we might think we can or should.

There are thirty-three spreads in this book: twelve full-moon spreads, twelve dark-moon spreads, four spreads for the fire festivals, four spreads for the equinoxes and the solstices, and one spread for the blue moon (full moon number thirteen), the Fool of the lunar cycle. Diagrams of each spread are included to illustrate how to lay out the cards and to hint at how they might communicate with each other as they are put down. The shapes made by the cards (e.g., square, triangle, V, or /\) also provide hints as to how the cards speak, because they show how the energy flows from the first card to the next, to the next, and so on. The sample spreads illustrate what a completed layout looks like and include a write-up of how the cards answer the questions posed by the particular spread. Each reader's spread will be different, of course, but sometimes it helps to have an example when you're just getting started.[2]

Speaking of getting started, since this book follows the Gregorian or Western calendar, it begins with the month of January and follows all the way through to December. The fire festivals, equinoxes, and solstices are placed within the book based on approximately where they fall on the calendar (e.g.,

2 Please note that some of the sample readings mention the colors that are present in the cards, which you will not be able to see if you are reading the print version of this book. Full-color images of the spreads are available in the ebook, which can be purchased at Microcosm.Pub/TarotYear with the coupon code TAROTEBOOK.

Imbolg comes before February, Lúnasa comes before August, and the Autumnal Equinox comes after September), just to keep things simple. Although this book is organized such that it starts in January, it's not at all necessary to wait until January 1 to begin using it. I am a big fan of beginning where you are in just about every aspect of life, and that holds true for this book. So, for example, if you pick up a copy just after the Dark Moon of September, start there, and then just circle back to the beginning of the book when January arrives. If you would prefer to wait until January 1 to begin, though, that's ok too. And if you want to begin at Samhain, considered by many practitioners to be the beginning of the witch's year, please do so. This book is meant to be a tool of discovery, and the best place to begin any journey is right where you are in this moment. It is written to be useful to all Tarot enthusiasts, wherever they are on their journey. Enough explanations and descriptions are included to make the process clear for beginners, while those more familiar with the Tarot and working with different types of spreads can make use of the descriptions or not, as it suits them.

While the book is organized according to the flow of the calendar in the Northern Hemisphere, each draw includes a section for how to proceed with the reading if you're in the Southern Hemisphere. If you live below the equator, it's understandable to adopt an approach of doing the opposite of what's happening in the Northern Hemisphere, but things are more complex than that. There are questions for how to approach each reading in the Southern Hemisphere that may go beyond the "hot/cold" or "summer/winter" opposition dynamics, and it's my hope that readers in the Southern Hemisphere find useful ideas and spreads in this book as easily as their northern cousins might.

Each chapter begins with a section that describes themes, ideas, and questions to consider for that time of year. The spreads included in each chapter are described in brief. For each month, there is one spread for the full moon and one for the dark moon. The full moon spreads explore each month's possibilities for expansion, growth, flowing outward, and in general looking at how one exists in the world and in community. The dark moon spreads explore the more inward-looking side of things—how one engages with oneself—and may invite a clear look at one's shadow side, with regard to both how one deals with oneself and how one deals with others.

The book ends with a wild card spread for the blue moon, because as we travel through the calendar year, sometimes we get a blue moon (and don't worry, we'll talk more about what exactly a blue moon is). In this spread you can engage with the Celestial Fool, the Trickster, the wild card that might show you the way to exactly what you want or that might trip you up just for the heck of it. That's what wild cards do, right?

Recording your observations as you work through these spreads is a personal choice. Keeping a notebook can be useful because it will allow you to track how often certain cards come up and what their context is. For example, if you are consistently getting the Devil card in spread positions meant to reflect what you're not seeing that can hurt you, you might want to explore the possibility that you have a blindness toward your own weaknesses that's getting in your way. This sort of tracking can also be useful for determining whether a certain suit comes up a lot (e.g., if you consistently get a lot of Cups or Vessels cards during dark moons, perhaps you're being guided to look more closely at your emotional shadow self and how it's affecting your actions in the light of day). However, all that being said, if you prefer not to track your draws in the spread, that's ok too. It's up to you.

Before going too much further into the process, let's talk decks for a minute. These spreads are designed to be used with the Tarot, but if you have a favorite oracle deck you enjoy using, or for any other reason the Tarot just doesn't resonate with you, please feel free to use a different type of deck instead. Just note that the sample readings included in this book use a Tarot deck, so write-ups and explanations will all reference Tarot structure and symbology.

And if you do use a Tarot deck, you don't need to use a specific kind. The spreads will work with all types of Tarot and oracle decks, although the spreads included in this book use a deck built around the Rider-Waite-Smith model. Without going too far into the history-of-the-Tarot weeds, the difference between these types of decks involves symbology and the representation of those symbols, especially in the Minor Arcana portion of the deck.[3] Rider-Waite-Smith-style decks include images, figures, and symbols to explain the meaning of the card in story form, while the Tarot de Marseilles and Thoth Tarot decks stick to symbols reflecting the suit and number of the card in question and leave the "story" or meaning of the card to the cartomancer's memory and intuition. No one deck is better or more appropriate for the work laid out in this book than any other; it's entirely a matter of personal preference.

If you're new to the Tarot and are unsure what Tarot deck to use for your explorations, my advice would be to begin with a deck you are drawn to. You may have heard that you should only use decks that have been given to you, but that's a Tarot Old Wives' Tale and is untrue. Go to your local metaphysical shop or bookstore or find an online retailer to see which deck jumps out at you, and use that. And if no decks jump out at you, you can't go wrong with the Rider-Waite-Smith Tarot deck. It is approachable and direct, with clear images on each card that

---

3 "Minor Arcana" refers to the four suits of cards in a Tarot deck that most often represent the elements of Earth, Air, Fire, and Water. The name of each suit will depend on the deck (e.g., Air can be Swords, Quills, Aether, or anything else representing the mind, communication, and clarity). The Major Arcana comprises twenty-one trump cards that represent different archetypal energies (e.g., although both represent other things as well, we can say that at heart, the Hierophant represents spiritual authority on earth and the Emperor represents secular authority on Earth).

illustrate its meaning and message. As for using your Tarot deck, you may be wondering whether or not a ritual is required—some form of divination magic to enhance your reading. The simple answer is no, but you can perform a ritual if you want. There are many highly skilled Tarot readers who don't tap into the cards as a spiritual tool or practice, and that's absolutely fine. My way, though, is different in that I do use the cards as part of a regular spiritual practice. I'm going to share my ritual with you here, in case you're interested in starting a spiritual divination practice of your own. I am an animist, a polytheist, and an individual practitioner of Northern Heathen ways. You don't need to be any of those things to use this ritual though. Please feel free to adjust it to suit your own practice, gods, ancestors, and spirit guides and guardians.

A TAROT DIVINATION RITUAL

What You Need

- A candle—light-colored is best (yellow, gold, white, pastels); dark blue or indigo will work too, because it is associated with the Third Eye and is good for activating intuition. You'll also need the means to light the candle.

- Incense, Florida water, holy water, smoke stick, or herbal wand—this will be used to create sacred space.

- Your divination deck.

- A small offering dish—this can be anything that keeps liquids separate. It doesn't need to be fancy or even a dish, if you don't have one. When making offerings to my ancestors, I use recycled bottle caps.

- A notebook or journal to record the cards and any notes about the spread you're using.

What To Do

- Start by lighting the candle.

- Take a few deep, centering breaths to ground yourself in your space.

- Cast a circle of protection around yourself. There are many ways to do this; the simple way I describe here is what works for me. If you're using smoke to clear your circle, now is the time to light it and hold it up as you turn from one direction to the next. If you're using water, spray or spritz the water outward as you turn. Pick one of the four directions to start with (north, south, east, or west). I use east because that's where the sun rises and my day begins. Face east and say, "Sacred Powers of the East, I pray, please bless and protect my work today." Then turn to the right and face the south. Say, "Sacred Powers of the South, I pray, please bless and protect my work today." Then turn to the right, to the west, and say, "Sacred Powers of the West, I pray, please bless and protect my work today." Finally, turn to the right one more time, to the north, and say, "Sacred Powers of the North, I pray, please bless and protect my work today." As you turn in a circle addressing the directions, let your smoke stick or water spray flow in that direction, essentially creating a circle around yourself and where you will be doing your divination.

- The next piece of the ritual is personal and will depend on where you are in your practice, whether there are gods or spirits you already work with, and whether you have an active ancestor practice. The idea is to call on your helpers and guides to work with you as you work with the cards. In my practice, I call on Hekate first. She is a Greek goddess of the keys, of magic and witches and the crossroads. It's often useful to call upon the Ones who guard the crossroads first, I find, because they manage passage, pathways between spaces, roads coming in and roads going out, and making sure messages come through loud and clear and don't get lost between Point A and Point B. After calling upon Hekate with a prayer, I call upon the other gods and ancestors of my practice. I offer each one of them something: water for Hekate, juniper smoke for Frigg, a roll of the dice for Odin, perfume for Freya, road-opening oil for the Cailleach, crocheting for the Norns, water for a Sami water being I work with, and a prayer for my Disir. You may not have the time or inclination to go that deep with your offerings. If you prefer to keep it simple, you can pour some fresh water into your offering dish and offer it to your gods, guides, and helpers with a prayer acknowledging them and asking for their help with your work. It's always a good practice to remember to say "please" and "thank you"; the gods, guardians, and ancestors don't like having orders barked at them any more than you would.

- Now it's time to get your deck and the spread you'll be working with and get to work. Open to the spread you want to use and keep it handy. Shuffle your deck and offer whatever prayers you usually do or say whatever words you use when you shuffle—or just shuffle the cards, if that's your practice. As you do so, review the "Questions to Ponder" section of the spread you're doing to give yourself questions to consider as you read the cards. Then cut the cards and draw the number you need for the spread you're using. Keep track of the order in which you draw the cards from the deck, because the spreads rely on the card-draw sequence. Lay them out according to the spread diagram. If you've laid them out face down, turn them face up. You can do this one card at a time or turn them all at once. It's up to you. To guide your interpretation of the cards, look to the "Positions" section below the diagram, which states the questions that each card is answering for you.

- In your notebook, take note of anything that pops up for you: words, ideas, color associations, music, memories, and anything else that comes up. After you've completed your reading, thank the gods, guides, and anyone else you called in to help. In my practice, I name them all in reverse order (in other words, when I cast my circle I begin with Hekate and go through to my ancestors, so when I close the circle I start with my ancestors and end with Hekate). I say "thank you" into the flame of the candle so that when I blow it out, my words will be carried up in the candle's smoke.

As I mention above, spiritual use of the Tarot is a personal choice and not necessary to using the cards, so it's up to you as to whether to proceed down that road. It's been my choice to engage with the gods and my ancestors as much as I can with the cards, and I hope some of that comes through on the pages that follow.

Now let's pick up our notebooks and our decks and see what the cards have to say!

January

THE FULL MOON

*T*he first full moon of the calendar year is sometimes called the Wolf Moon because, in the distant past, the howling of winter wolves at the edges of community was real and represented danger and the possibility of death at the hands of seasonal forces beyond our control. To our ancestors, "winter" may have meant deep snow, howling wind, no access to anything until the snow melted, and living off the stores you'd saved up from the previous seasons until it was both possible and safe to leave the security of home and village to start foraging, planting, and hunting again. While most of us may no longer have to deal with packs of wolves in the woods outside our villages, this is still the time of year in the Northern Hemisphere when darkness falls early and leaves us huddled in our homes for warmth and security as danger in whatever form lurks outside our walls. These days winter might not translate into such a wild and lonesome existence, but at the Wolf Moon we're reminded of our most basic needs and desires and what we are required to do to meet them.

Whether you live in a place where it's very cold in January or not, you undoubtedly have experienced what it's like to feel deprived. Choices are a little harder, tempers a little sharper, and even the outer landscapes of the world take on a harsher edge than they might otherwise have when times are good. Things appear more black and white during these times, and danger may be less of an intellectual concept and more of a functional reality when we experience deprivation. We think of ourselves and our families first, putting the clan before outsiders as our thinking patterns get narrower. It's understandable that this happens: we want to make sure that our children are warm and safe, that our elders are fed and well cared for, and that we ourselves have the food, clothing, medicine, and shelter we need to keep the wolves at bay—whether those wolves are the actual predators of ancestral nightmares or a metaphor for what keeps us awake at night in modern times. This spread is designed to help you see where the wolves are in your life, how you're using or misusing precious resources, and how you can better take care of yourself and your loved ones during a dark time.

The Full Moon—Southern Hemisphere

Winter and the dark edges of the calendar won't come up for you at this time, but the issues could very well be the same. Instead of isolation caused by cold, wind, or snow, you might be dealing with different kinds of deprivation. When the sun is blazing, is it water that's scarce? Or shade? Is it not snow that traps you in your home but the unrelenting sun? Has wildfire become a real threat that cannot be controlled in the same way that a blizzard cannot be? When you ask yourself what kind of summer wolves are at your door, consider that they may be in sheep's clothing.

THE DARK MOON

Reflected though it might be, the light cast by the moon when it hangs above us in the night sky still gives us at least some way of perceiving what faces us in the surrounding darkness. When it vanishes every month it leaves us to our own devices, pondering who we are when everything else is stripped away. In January, when we're facing the cold and hunger of deep winter, the dark moon brings an added layer of questioning and uncertainty to a month already full of questions. When working with the energies of the January full moon, we try to see how we fit in, how we're able to reconcile our individual needs with those of the wider community. But when the January moon is dark, we face our shadow selves and try to see who we are in the darkness. We summon the courage to work with the questions that bring us close to the edge of the abyss within; we see with our inner eyes because our physical eyes won't serve us now.

The Dark Moon—Southern Hemisphere
In midsummer, when life is still loud and bright during the darkest night, can we even see ourselves in the fierce, persistent light? The dark moons are excellent opportunities to practice seeing in the dark, to acknowledge the person everyone else sees while pushing past that in order to bring up our shadow self that hides in the dark. Who are we when the only light we can see by is a pale reflection of what's real?

JANUARY FULL MOON
Keywords
Cold, hunger, the wild within, individuality

Questions to Ponder
Consider the following as you shuffle your deck. How do we deal with deprivation and hunger? When times are lean, how do we protect our resources? What is our connection with the wildness within? Does "safety" mean a kind of rugged individuality or a communal existence? How do we see ourselves carrying forward the necessary tasks we've laid out for ourselves with our new resolutions? How does danger manifest itself in our lives?

Spread
After shuffling, draw nine cards and lay them out according to the following diagram.

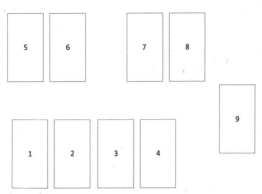

Positions

1. ***What is my real situation right now? Are things better or worse than I think?*** This is a time for being unfailingly real with yourself. See clearly and without romance or sentiment or drama. You know that biting, scouring wind outside? Or that blizzard you've seen on internet videos that blasts across the Siberian tundra or the parking lots of football stadiums in Buffalo, New York? When you think about your real situation, be as clear and uncompromising as that wind. You're not doing yourself any favors by dramatizing things. If your situation is good, that's great! Let's work with that. If it's dire, we can work with that, too. But let's see it for what it is.

2. ***What is my biggest resource drain?*** Here's another opportunity to be as clear-eyed as possible without blaming anyone. Look at what your resources are and where they're going. It doesn't have to be a bad thing— all cars need fuel of some kind, and we don't go around blaming them every time we fill up. We need food and water to survive as well. So where is most of your money going, or your time, or whatever resource is being most drained and not being replenished? Maybe it's not what you think. Maybe you've put so much focus on one area

of life that you *think* is taking it all out of you that you're missing the real drain. So let's identify what's really going on.

3. ***What is my greatest need right now?*** This one could be as simple as "to win the lottery," or it could be much more complex. Do you need help managing your resources? Do you need to stop buying lottery tickets and start a savings account with that money instead? Maybe you need to be less practical and more whimsical as a way of drawing the energy of abundance to you, or perhaps you need to face what's really driving your overspending. Use this card to see beyond the obvious.

4. ***What hidden resources do I have?*** Speaking of seeing beyond the obvious, we tend to overlook resources that are right in front of us—resources that often don't manifest until we need them most. Maybe you have a skill you didn't realize you had, and now's the time to start developing it. Maybe you're much better positioned now to explore other opportunities (e.g., going back to school or taking a class, getting a certification, learning a language, or turning a hobby into a hustle) than you were ten years ago, but you've gotten so bogged down in your routine that it doesn't seem possible. Now's a good time to jail-break that hidden resource and see what you can do with it!

5. ***Who and/or where are the wolves (the danger) in my life?*** Nobody really wants to look at this—of course they don't. Who among us wants to think that people we know or situations we're in might actually be harmful? But it's valuable information to have. Open your mind to the possibility that there might be dangers in places you least expect. It's better to know about them before they do harm than after.

6. *What is the storm in my life right now, the thing I can't control?* It would be so valuable to everyone to be able to identify when and where damage is going to hit; but how to handle the storm, how to ride it out once it's struck, might just be the next best thing. Here we look at what the uncontrollable forces are in our lives and how to ride them out without falling to pieces. It's useful to know that if there's some wild thing happening in our lives at the moment, we might not actually be able to control it. I know parents of toddlers who can speak very well to this: you think you can control something so small and seemingly helpless, but when it gets going, when it reveals itself as a true force of nature, the best thing to do is to let the tantrum happen and get out of the way. Where can we take a second look at something in our lives that we think is easily managed but is in fact way beyond us and needs to be left alone to run its course?

7. *What advice do you have to help me make it through?* Ask your ancestors, your spirit team, your gods, guides, and guardians, for their best advice for making it through. If the issue is personal and deeply human, such as managing addiction or handling lean times, focus on your ancestors or guides who have lived human lives and know what it's like. Something else important to remember: If advice is offered, it's up to you whether or not to take it. We've all got free will here.

8. *What lessons can I learn from this time of deprivation?* This is another opportunity to take a hard, clear-eyed look at where you are and what got you here. Many times it won't have been anything you did or didn't do; often forces beyond our control govern our choices or at least narrow the field of options available to us (think about

the Great Recession of 2008, for example). But where are the lessons we *can* learn? What are the areas in which our actions shaped our current outcome, and how can we use this information to influence our future days? And even considering those times when global forces were on full display (for example, when the Covid-19 pandemic seriously impacted international business, travel, and public health), what can we learn about how to manage our resources better going forward?

9. ***Give me some good news, please.*** It's always possible to ask for some good news, and there's nothing wrong with ending on a high note. What good has come of the current situation (if it was negative in the first place), or what good will come of it going forward? This is a perfect opportunity to practice releasing expectations of what's to come. Maybe the good news will be as simple as "the sun will rise tomorrow." But how much more powerful a sign of hope could there be? Where there's life, there's hope. Where there's hope, there's possibility. Possibility changes lives, so let's see where the possibility is for change here, for learning and growth and using what we've learned to our best advantage in the days and weeks to come.

Sample Reading

It's always kind of funny to me when the 3 of Cups shows up next to the Devil. It's like the Tarot is showing us the party the night before and the walk of shame the next day. And it's not just the party in the top right; this spread shows a lot of cards connecting and talking to each other. There is heart-based energy that's reflected in the 3 of Swords and the 5 of Cups, the Queen of Pentacles speaks to the 4 of Wands and the Ace of Pentacles both, and we have two 2s speaking to each other of balance and movement: the 2 of Wands and the 2 of Pentacles.

1. ***What is my real situation right now?*** The 5 of Cups, a card of disappointment and loss. The key is to acknowledge and release what's gone and focus on what remains.

2. ***What is my biggest resource drain?*** The 3 of Swords, an indicator of mental anguish, which in this position emphasizes the 5 of Cups. Our biggest resource drain is our own mind.

3. ***What is my greatest need right now?*** The Queen of Pentacles, who tells us to get back into our bodies. We need to be present to solve our problems.

4. ***What hidden resources do I have?*** The 2 of Wands, here a "resources" card of balance, cooperation, and command, and an indicator of huge potential when engaging with others.

5. ***Who and/or where are the wolves (the danger) in my life?*** The Ace of Pentacles, which is the life force here in

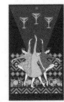

the manifest realm, showing us that the danger lies in our material resources (e.g., our money, housing, food). But it's small and manageable, so deal with it early, before it gets out of control.

6. *What is the storm in my life right now, the thing I can't control?* The 4 of Wands, showing us storms around home, family, and that which is closest to us.

7. *What advice do you have to help me make it through?* The 3 of Cups. The advice from the ancestors is "furious dancing." The worse things get, the more important it is to reach out to one another and smile.

8. *What lessons can I learn from this time of deprivation?* The Devil, who shows us where we're not seeing things clearly. We've been engaging in wishful thinking, perhaps, when hard-headed practicality would be much more useful.

9. *Give me some good news, please.* The 2 of Pentacles. We will be successful when we start small and focus on the day-to-day work in front of us. Step-by-step is the way to go.

JANUARY DARK MOON

Keywords
Identity, courage, fear, self versus community

Questions to Ponder
Consider the following as you shuffle your deck. Who are we when we're alone in the dark? When there's nothing to see by, what is our guide? Do we summon the courage we need, or do we crumple in fear? Where does the courage come from? Are we alone as we

pass through the darkness, or do we have unseen allies? Do we numb ourselves to the journey? Are we walking into a trap?

Spread

After shuffling, draw four cards and lay them out according to the following diagram.

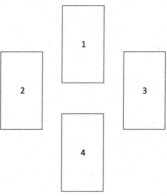

Positions

1. ***What will light my path right now?*** When in the dark, it's completely normal to reach for some source of light. Where is that light source for you? Is it the same now as it was a year ago? Ten years ago? When you were a child? Are you aware of the light source, or is it something that you take for granted?

2. ***What am I not seeing that can help me?*** Are there allies around you that you're not aware of? There probably are, so focus on where they might be. They might be something (or someone) you haven't thought of or noticed before; they might not even be human! There might be spirit allies who have come to help you through a specific time, or plant or animal allies who carry wisdom you can share.

3. ***What am I not seeing that can hurt me?*** When I was in college many years ago, I broke my arm when I slipped off a curb and fell into the street. The curb was barely four inches high, but I didn't see it and slipped right off as I stepped onto what I thought was the street. The break was only a fracture, so the campus doctor didn't set it, and because of that, to this day I have pain in that arm whenever the barometric pressure in my environment shifts. That's a literal example of not seeing something that can hurt you (for decades afterwards, in my case!), but not all pitfalls have to be quite so literal. Are you heading for a different kind of fall that could be avoided if only you could see far enough ahead?

4. ***Who am I when all else is stripped away?*** This is one of the most valuable questions we can face, and we face it and perhaps come up with different answers many times in our lives. We all put on roles, masks, different faces to help us through situations, challenges, and difficulties throughout our lives, but if we don't get into the practice of taking those masks off, we may forget how. And if we forget how to be authentic, we will be without access to our most valuable asset: ourselves.

Sample Reading

Our spread shows us rootedness and roundedness, with more Earth energy from the Pentacles than anything else. There's only one court card, and that one a Page, the most youthful and inexperienced of the court cards. This is young energy, close to the ground, thoughtful but focused on what we're looking at and what is real.

1. ***What will light my path right now?*** The 6 of Swords. We have to move on to energize our creativity and courage, to discover a new source of light. What has worked in the past won't work now.

2. ***What am I not seeing that can help me?*** The Page of Wands. We're more of a beginner right now than we think, so let go of all those things everybody else says you should think or believe or do and write your own! Also, the Page as messenger can *literally* be a messenger, so this card in this position is a good prompt to look around in our lives and see where we're getting our information.

3. ***What am I not seeing that can hurt me?*** The 7 of Pentacles, a card of methodical, process-based growth, development, and analysis of what is and isn't working, shows us that the current way we're doing things isn't helping and we need to try something else.

4. ***Who am I when all else is stripped away?*** The Ace of Pentacles. We are the spark of manifestation, which means at this time we can make whatever we want.

Imbolg

Keywords
Birth, new fire, emergence, hearth-fire

*I*mbolg is the first fire festival of the calendar year and is celebrated by some as a New Year festival because it falls so close to the Lunar New Year. It is therefore a celebration of beginnings, of new things, and, in some cases, of actual pregnancy and the promise of new life that will be born soon. "Imbolg" is an Irish word meaning "in the belly," referring to pregnancy and the imminence of new life. In the northern half of the world, the days, which have been getting longer since Yule, are noticeably lighter now and the sun is starting to strengthen during the day. Winter's grip is beginning to weaken. The creeks and rivers start to flow a little faster as the snow and ice begin to melt, and trees and plants start to sprout new buds. There are even flowers starting to appear here and there, although winds still blow powerful and cold.

This is the perfect time to start thinking about cleaning out the old and making plans for spring. It may not be practical to start our spring cleaning early, but we can certainly start planning. It's also a good time to light candles and honor the winter gods and goddesses who have seen us through the darkest of the dark days. The Celtic goddess Brigid is especially honored on or around Imbolg, depending upon the tradition. Priestesses of Brigid guard Her eternal flame every other day of the year and hold special vigils through the night on the eve of Imbolg, making sure that the fire—which represents life, hearth, and home—never goes out. Brigid is hearth fire, but She is also honored for the songs and stories we tell as we keep ourselves connected and bound to each other through the winter—the fire of creativity, poetry, and the living word of the gods in the hearts of the people.

Questions to Ponder

Consider the following as you shuffle your deck. What new plans and projects do we want to give birth to? What skills do we want to develop? What signs are there around us that life has found a way forward? What is our "hearth fire" that must never be allowed to go out? What is emerging in ourselves and the world around us?

Southern Hemisphere

If you live in the Southern Hemisphere, the holiday you will be celebrating at this time is Lúnasa (or Lammas). Feel free to go to the Lúnasa spread to work with those energies where you are, or you may continue on here if you prefer.

You may notice the light beginning to shift. Changes are happening faster and faster each day. What is emerging? What lessons have been pushing you for the past few months, and how do you feel yourself changing from their effects?

Spread

After shuffling, draw seven cards and lay them out according to the following diagram.

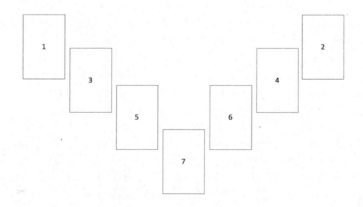

Positions

1. *How can I best tap into the energy of Imbolg?* Because this is a special day, it's a wonderful opportunity to dial in to the special energies that are only available on this day. Promise, potentialities, beginnings, the protection of the most precious thing—all of these themes tap into Imbolg and resonate profoundly today.

2. *What do I need to do to make the best and safest home for that which I'm currently bringing into being?* Sometimes it's very easy to forget that our environment affects us in many ways. Do we need to clear things out? Or do we need to add a missing element to our space to increase the sense of safety and security? This card will help point out areas in which we can make room for that new thing we're trying to create, whether it's by clearing out our physical space, processing some old feelings and releasing grief, or perhaps adding security lights outside our front door. It could even represent getting to know our neighbors better, creating a safe community around ourselves not only for us but for those around us.

3. *What is most dangerous right now for both me and that which is emerging?* Is it possible to know in advance where danger comes from? Not always, but if there is a dangerous element within our space, it's best to do what we can to identify it so that we can take appropriate action. In this card we identify that element or elements that will be in conflict with us and our new idea or project or way of being, so that we can clear it out of our space as much as possible—or be on the lookout for it if it attempts to make any kind of comeback.

4. *What new skills can I develop to best help myself?* Sometimes the best way to prove to ourselves that we're ready for something new is to practice a new habit that is

in alignment with it. For example, if we want to develop a healthier lifestyle, a first step would be to quit smoking so that our body and lungs are in better shape to support us as we exercise more. Or if we want to write a novel or create any other kind of art, it might be a good idea to start by making some "artist" time in our calendar every week, or even every day if possible. There may be things we need to let go of, but by doing so we're proving to ourselves that we're ready to take this new commitment seriously.

5. *What do I need to release?* In the same vein as the previous card, now is the time for us to consider what we can let go of in order to make room for the new, emerging energy of Imbolg. We've got time yet, so there's no need to cut things out immediately or do anything similarly drastic. But it's a good time to start identifying those things that no longer support the new path and energy. It's not the same as with the card in the third position, which helps us identify those things that are actively working against us and are therefore dangerous to us and the new energy we are trying to support and create. This is more like creating space by removing old, stale activities and possibly even relationships that have become more of a burden than a joy.

6. *Who or what is my midwife?* When birthing anything, we need help. I can't imagine choosing to give birth to a baby without help, although more power to those who do! For those who choose to seek help, the midwife card points us to the best possible source of aid. It can be a person or a place or maybe even an animal or plant spirit that is aligned with our new project. Or perhaps it is an idea or new way of thinking and perceiving the world that will help us bring our project to life when the

time comes. Again, there's time yet, so it's wise to use this opportunity to seek out help and create relationships before we actually find ourselves in a place where we need them.

7. ***What is emerging?*** This may seem like an obvious one, especially if the project we're working on is a new baby or a new home or even a new job. But sometimes our desire for something—anything—new is not clear; we don't know what we want, we just know that we need something other than what we have. So when the opportunity arises to work with the energy of Imbolg, it makes sense to ask what can be manifested out of our current reality. What is possible? What can we make with the ingredients we have?

Sample Reading

When we look at this spread as a whole, we have loads of Water (Cups) and Air (Swords) and no Earth (Pentacles) or Fire (Wands), indicating that emotional and intellectual truth are showing up in the spread without too much concern about grounding it all in the material world. We also have an interesting mix of Minor Arcana cards—three court cards and three pips ("pips" is an old-fashioned name for the Ace through 10 of any deck of cards). There's a balance between focused, individualized energy brought in by the court cards—as if they may be speaking directly to or about people we know, or reflecting aspects of ourselves and where we are in our journey—and the more common life experiences represented by the 7, the 6, and the 2.

1. ***How can I best tap into the energy of Imbolg?*** The Page of Swords. We are being called to begin from the beginning, slow down, and plan. Imbolg is not only about new beginnings, but is also a time to honor family, ancestry, and our connection to the unseen. Wisdom is

knowledge plus experience, so get help from those wiser and more experienced than you.

2. *What do I need to do to make the best and safest home for that which I'm currently bringing into being?* The 7 of Cups tells us we have to choose what to keep and what to release as we make our home ready for the new arrival.

3. *What is most dangerous right now for both me and that which is emerging?* The Queen of Swords—as we move into a new way of being or take on new projects, people will pop out of the woodwork with all their ideas and opinions. Take what resonates as wisdom here and leave the rest. Practice as much discernment as possible.

4. *What new skills can I develop to best help myself?* The 6 of Swords, a card of movement into new ways of thinking, perceiving, and understanding. As the energy of Imbolg rises around us, we can start looking for new ways to see both ourselves and our environment.

5. *What do I need to release?* The 2 of Cups, which says that over-romanticizing things won't help. What we might be trying to create in the world will come to pass, but relying on others to provide resources or solutions could be a mistake.

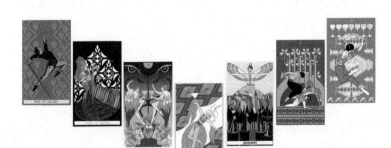

6. ***Who or what is my midwife?*** Judgment. This card is about preparation, about doing what needs to be done to be finished with a cycle. Imbolg is the first of the major holidays along the great Wheel of the Year, so it closes off the energy of the previous cycle and opens the door for the new one.

7. ***What is emerging?*** The Page of Cups. The gentle sweetness of the energy coming in needs protection, safety, and strong boundaries to grow within. This is our heart's blood.

February

THE FULL MOON

*T*he full moon in February is sometimes called the "Snow Moon" because of the weather in the Northern Hemisphere, but also because of what snow signifies: there is a silence and separation from community in snowy climates, a muffling of the noise from outside and an increasing sense of isolation from within. Climates can be harsh in February, not just for the cold but for a sense of the relentlessness of winter. If it doesn't snow where you are, maybe it rains. Or perhaps there is relentless drought. California has had many drought-dry winters in the last forty years, and the total lack of moisture in winter—when the state usually gets most of its rain—can lend a desperate vibe to even the cheeriest Valentine's Day party.

There can be a sense of lack, or an *actual* lack, during this full moon, a feeling of belt-tightening and hanging in there until spring begins to make herself known. Anything we've saved up from the previous year might be gone by this time, like savings depleted after the winter holidays. So it's even more important now than at other times of the year to look for the joy, the inspiration, the goodness in the world around us. In the United States we celebrate Black History Month in February, honoring the contributions of African Americans to our national story and history and facing the reality of how deeply embedded our national foundations are in the profound injustice of slavery. Wherever we are, whatever our history is, learning who we are as humans, speaking up for the truth, and honoring justice are things to celebrate. Finding ways to learn and grow from the necessities of life is one of those valuable practices that teach us more about ourselves than joyful, happy times ever can. So we turn to the Snow Moon to help us expand these thoughts and ideas, even as we do our winter gut checks; we look at our relationships through the lens of necessity, truth, history, and where we fit into community.

The Full Moon—Southern Hemisphere

How do you deal with and process necessity and lack in your life? Where do you go when things get difficult? Where do you find joy in hard times? Are there edges of your history that need to be explored and documented? What part of your story has the world never heard?

THE DARK MOON

It's not too great a challenge to imagine the constraining power of the dark moon during February, when it's already the depths of winter in the Northern Hemisphere. While spring might be just around the corner, it's not here yet. The earth is still frozen, the month is short so paychecks might be lighter than usual, and if we're surrounded by people in love happily celebrating Valentine's Day while we're having ramen and beer alone and binge-watching reality television, things might be feeling a little grim. Maybe we're even remembering that we should probably start getting our annual income taxes underway, and if that's not an occasion for an extra can of beer and some crushed Cheetos on that ramen, nothing is.

Perhaps you can tell that my go-to when things get tough is food. Not particularly good food either, but food that's salty and crunchy, with just enough gluten-free ingredients to make me feel better about blowing up my diet. We all have our go-tos to help us get by, and we can take the opportunity during this dark moon to examine them and how they run our lives if we let them take over when we're down. We can also look at where we can learn from them and move ourselves into a better place to take healthier advantage of spring when it arrives. We can look at how we deal with these compulsive behaviors, little or big, and we can see where we're pushing responsibility for our own problems onto others instead of doing the work that needs to be done to heal ourselves. Because, at their core, that's what these dark moons are all about: finding ways to heal ourselves so that we can grow from our shadow lessons and move beyond the "wounded healer" space.

The Dark Moon—Southern Hemisphere

Addictions are addictions, and demons are demons, whether it's pitch black outside in the depths of winter or bright sunlight on the longest day of the year. While it might seem more intuitive to face our demons and unhealthy impulses when we're in literal darkness, on sunnier days you can still take the time to look within and call up those energies that help you hide or cause you to numb out. As your northern kin are looking for that spark of light in the darkness, you can see how your relationship with that spark thrives or withers in the full light of day. Do you find yourself needing shelter from the sun? Sometimes that's the only sensible place to be in summer, but there comes a time when "sheltering" becomes "hiding," and this dark moon can be a good time to examine that duality.

FEBRUARY FULL MOON

Keywords

Challenge, cold, facing difficulty

Questions to Ponder

Consider the following as you shuffle your deck. What is the truth of our situation right now? How do we handle silence? What seeds of the future are in our possession, even now when everything else has been used up? What can we draw inspiration from, and where can we learn from the past? What do we need to honor and pay our respects to, especially if it's something that has been in our blind spot up until now? Look around you and try to visualize the truth of where you are right now and where you want to be in the future. Be as honest as you can and think things through as much as possible. Ask yourself the questions you need to ask, and be ready to hear the answers (as much as any of us can ever be ready).

Spread

After shuffling, draw five cards and lay them out according to the following diagram.

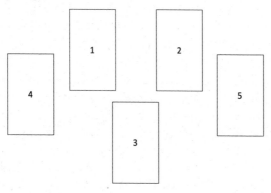

Positions

1. ***What is the truth of my situation right now?*** While it's always valuable to see the hopeful side of any situation, sometimes being real with yourself about what isn't working and what isn't realistic is just as valuable. What is most necessary in your life? Where do you draw the line between "want" and "need," or do you draw that line at all? Let the cards tell you the truth about what you're facing, rather than simply hearing what you want to hear.

2. ***What do I need to honor?*** Is there something in your life right now that you haven't been paying enough attention to, or that you've perhaps been taking for granted? Where are the holes in your integrity? Where can you start to see your own culpability in any social blindness about

what the world is really like for others, and how can you begin to pay proper respect and make offerings that will serve all, including yourself?

3. *What can I draw inspiration from?* What is in your world right now that can inspire you, if you let it? Where do you get ideas? Is there something different you can try? Where are you being pulled to sample a different energy? Are you resisting trying something new because it's unfamiliar? Where can you find the strength and courage to walk through a new door that might just change your life?

4. *What can I learn from the past?* Here's an interesting thing about the past: everybody has a story and a point of view. Everybody has a way of seeing things and an understanding of common events. Is there something you've missed as your worldview developed? What treasures of understanding and compassion are out there just waiting to be discovered? Where are you not looking that needs your direct attention, and how can you best access it?

5. *What are the seeds of future harvest?* Of all the things left to you at this moment, what can you begin planting for the next harvest season? If you want to be somewhere six, nine, or twelve months from now, how can you act today to move toward that goal? Have you experienced any sort of lack or necessity this February that you don't want to go through again next year? How can you plan to avoid reliving that experience?

Sample Reading

The presence of only Minor Arcana cards in this spread indicates on at least one level that the work that needs to be done during this full moon is of the day-to-day variety—the work of living and being and getting through day by day by day. While the Major Arcana can tell us what it means to be human, the Minor Arcana can tell us how to be human and how we're doing at it.

1. *What is the truth of my situation right now?* The 6 of Cups is a card often associated with nostalgia and childhood and what that means for us now, indicating a need to look at where we came from because it's leaking into our lives at the present moment. How can we make choices for ourselves now that will send a message to our inner selves that they are valuable, shielded, and protected?

2. *What do I need to honor?* The 3 of Wands, a card of value returned, also indicates what work needs to be respected here. If we want to accomplish our goals and make it through whatever difficulty we might be experiencing, we have to buckle down and do the work. Honor the job.

3. *What can I draw inspiration from?* The 2 of Swords is a card of both friction and balance, a card of differences colliding, but also of peaceful acceptance of what is and what's possible if there are no limitations except our own inexperience or ignorance.

4. *What can I learn from the past?* The 5 of Swords speaks here of a lose-lose situation. Perhaps we're leaving something behind and the way it was left wasn't ideal. There are battles where the winners and losers are clear, and there are battles where in the end everything sucks and nobody comes out ahead.

5. *What are the seeds of future harvest?* The 7 of Cups is all about choices. Our seeds of the future will grow into what they will grow into; there's no knowing what they will become until they're grown. The best we can do is choose our path and get comfortable with the uncertainty of waiting.

FEBRUARY DARK MOON

Keywords
Bitterness, dealing with our demons, hiding

Questions to Ponder
Consider the following as you shuffle your deck. What are our go-tos when we want to numb out? Do we face our problems head-on, or do we take steps to outrun them? What can we do to start making friends with our demons, or at least try to turn them into allies or teachers? Where do we push all the wrong boundaries while allowing others to run roughshod over us? Do we dig ourselves into ever-deeper holes instead of practicing the art of stopping? Who are we when life gets hard? Let's check in with ourselves about our blind spots—we've all got them—and see what we can do about getting a bit of light into those spaces.

Spread

After shuffling, draw five cards and lay them out according to the following diagram.

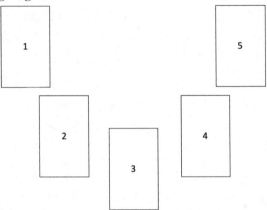

Positions

1. *What truth am I hiding from?* What's the big issue that I somehow keep looking away from rather than facing? This card can also reveal elements about why this issue is so hard to face and why it keeps coming up.

2. *What are my blinders made of?* This can be the "demon" card, providing a glimpse of whatever energies are most getting in the way of us stepping forward into the light that has dawned with Imbolg earlier in the month. Even if you know what your addictions and compulsions are, you might be surprised. In the same way that an eating disorder is more about control than it is about food, your blinders could represent something deeper than the actual behavior itself. While it's important to discover what we're not seeing, it's almost more important to learn why we're not seeing it in the first place.

3. *What tools do I already have that can help me face uncomfortable reality?* How can I learn to use them, or

if I already know how to use them, how can I become more skillful at it? And if I don't have the tools I need at all, where can I find them?

4. ***What's the best first step to take toward healing?*** Baby steps are what I'm talking about here. Sometimes if we're really afraid, just acknowledging what we're afraid of is huge. Or if we've been sitting with an issue for a while, perhaps we're ready to take the next step and we just need a little encouragement (or a gentle push).

5. ***What's my "Phial of Galadriel," my talisman that will help me shine and be most powerfully myself in the darkness?*** If you've read *The Lord of the Rings*, you know what I'm referring to. If not, the Phial of Galadriel is a gift given to the hero of the story to be a light in the darkness "when all other lights go out." It is a vessel of starlight sacred to the giver, and when he uses it, the hero of the story himself blazes not only with the light from the phial but also with the pure radiance of his own heart. It empowers him to trust himself and the magical world to which he's connected, just like we all are connected to this beautiful world we live in. What talisman can you draw upon when things are at their scariest, that can bring out your courage and your deepest belief in yourself?

Sample Reading

In this spread, we can see both our civilized selves (the World card) and our wild selves (the High Priestess), ancient pieces accessible to us when we get quiet and let ourselves tap into Source (whatever that is for each of us, whether it is our Higher Power, our concept of God, Goddess, or Godx, or the natural world as a living, sacred being). There are beginnings (the Ace of Cups) and endings as well, showing us how the entire journey can be contained within a single drop of water, a lifetime within a step.

1. *What truth am I hiding from?* The 2 of Wands is a card of mastery, dominion, and taking the bull by the horns. We are more in charge than we think we are, and it's time now to start doing something about it.

2. *What are my blinders made of?* The Ace of Cups is saying in no uncertain terms here that leading with the heart at all times is a mistake that drives us to make choices based on what we *want* to be true, what we *want* to believe, rather than what's actually facing us. Time for the rose-colored glasses to come off.

3. *What tools do I already have that can help me face uncomfortable reality?* The 6 of Wands is coming through as a powerful action card of great energy and forward movement. We need to start developing more action-oriented skills and fewer "sit and think" skills.

4. *What's the best first step to take toward healing?* The World represents the completion of a cycle, being done and being where you are. Listen to the wisdom coming in from all sides, but be prepared to let go of what has reached the end of its natural life. Don't cling to processes or events that are over.

5. *What's my "Phial of Galadriel," my talisman that will help me shine and be most powerfully myself in the*

darkness? The High Priestess is telling us here to stop listening to other people and how they do things. It's fine that other folks do things their own way, but it's also fine for us to do our own thing. Let your talisman be your sacred birthright as a human being: your sacred connection to Source.

March

THE FULL MOON

You know those days after big rainstorms when the ground is full of worms? I remember doing the March "Tiptoe Around All the Worms on the Street" dance as a kid—unless it was a drought year, and at those times I would wonder where the worms went. Then it would rain again and there they'd be, wiggling around in the street. I used to think they were drowning in the morning puddles, so I'd grab a stick and save as many as I could, probably to the great delight of every robin and scrub jay hopping around in the nearby trees, just waiting for a nice, tasty breakfast. It didn't occur to me until much later that the worms didn't appear every time after it rained, but only in the spring. The earth is beginning to warm up as spring approaches, so of course the worms would be coming up and getting flushed out of their earthy homes when the rains fell and softened the ground.

March can also be a time of wildly unpredictable weather. Where I live there's often a mini heat wave in March that lasts a few days and tricks us all into thinking spring (and maybe even summer) is finally here, and then it's freezing again a few days later—or as "freezing" as it gets near San Francisco. In the northeast part of the US, they say March "comes in like a lion and goes out like a lamb," referring to how the wild storms of late winter are followed by the gentle warmth of early spring. Depending on where you live, you can get the sense that the earth herself is literally waking up during this month. And when the moon is full, it's a perfect time to take energetic advantage of this expansion from all indoors, all the time, to it being ok (and maybe even advisable) to start opening the windows. Daffodils are blooming, and, depending on where you are, the cherry blossoms might be in the midst of their annual riot into every imaginable shade of pink. It's as if the Earth Mother is asking us, "Remember me, kids?" Of course, she exists in all seasons and asks us to remember her in the skeletal depths of winter, when she might be the last thing on our minds; but her voice can be easier to hear among the colors and sounds and even smells of spring. As the sun gets stronger and the water begins to flow more freely around us, as the birds celebrate their annual worm-a-palooza and the winds carry less ice and more fragrance, how do our own thoughts grow, expand, and take account of our responsibilities and opportunities for the blossoming year ahead?

The Full Moon—Southern Hemisphere

As the Great Wheel gets ready to turn at the equinox, do you feel the energies of the summer fading around you? What is changing as autumn and winter approach? Are there beings emerging from the shadows that demand to be noticed more now? As the last full moon of summer lights up the sky, in what ways can you best tap into the expansive energies of March to help you get ready for the coming darkness? What can you do to help yourself listen and really hear the messages from the world around you as the light begins to fade and the final harvest of the year approaches?

THE DARK MOON

When you feel flooded with excess, what do you do about it? When the rains come and wash away the grime and muck, what are you left with? What are you carrying that you're really fighting to leave behind? As spring blossoms all around us in the Northern Hemisphere, it's a good time to look at what's taking up too much energy, preventing all the new seeds we've discovered and developed throughout the winter from taking root and growing. In the dark of the moon is a good time for releasing energies; and in the face of March's turbulent weather, any of us can get a firm grip on what we want to release and fling it away for the wind to catch and carry. If you were able to give voice to the deep part of yourself that grasps what needs released and says, "I DON'T WANT THIS," what would she say after that? What are we too afraid to face but must so that we can process the last shreds of winter and move, with both feet and a full heart, into spring?

It's important to do this work, because moving through and beyond our personal crap matters when we look to start working on our community-and-society crap. Consider, for example, how some white Americans get defensive when told we need to acknowledge our inherent racism. We respond with words like, "My family never owned slaves," or "I've read a book by Audre Lord, so I *can't* be racist." That's a pretty low bar, but ok. That may be true. But I'm reminded of something I heard on an episode of CNN's program *United Shades of America.* The episode[4] was about reparations for slavery, and in it, W. Kamau Bell interviewed Nikole Hannah Jones, *New York Times* racial justice reporter and creator of the 1619 Project, who said that if a person can inherit wealth they can inherit debt. The truth of such a simple statement knocked the air out of my lungs for a few breaths. White Americans have a massive debt to repay, whether our individual ancestors owned slaves or not, and facing up to that reality is part of our national shadow work that we'd best be getting on with sooner rather than later. For those unfamiliar with the term, "shadow work" refers to work a person does to understand the dark side of their personality or psyche. Cleveland Clinic defines it as follows: "The idea of shadow work is that we all have parts of ourselves that we've repressed or largely ignored. Those long-forgotten aspects of our personalities, the parts of our identity that we've come to reject, make up our shadow self."

Doing any level of shadow work isn't pretty or easy, and it's not meant to be. Facing one's demons can be daunting. But it's important work, because it means that we can return to society after winter's solitude with an open heart and a willingness to

---

4 Season 5, episode 7, titled "Reparations."

communicate and cooperate, to learn and to grow. It can give us more room to expand into the next full moon, without packing around all that extra baggage that needs to get dissolved and released into the spring winds.

The Dark Moon—Southern Hemisphere

Fear is a universal human emotion, and using the energy of the dark moon to shift from fear to freedom is something that can be done anywhere, at any time. Ask yourself what forces are moving around you right now. Can you tap into them to help move the shadow energy you're working with? Is there moving water near you? Or a breezy park or hill? Even sitting in a room with a fan blowing will call in the energy of movement and change.

MARCH FULL MOON

Keywords

Thaw, spring, flushing-out, opportunism

Questions to Ponder

Consider the following as you shuffle your deck. What energy is rising up most powerfully right now? As the winter ice melts in the strengthening sun, what is being released? Are there energies hopping around like birds, just waiting to devour whatever has been flushed out by the winter rains of our lives? What do we need to protect as we plan our spring planting? As the last full moon of winter expands across the night sky, what tools can we use to best take advantage of the new life growing and beginning to bloom all around us?

Spread

After shuffling, draw four cards and lay them out according to the following diagram.

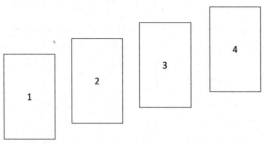

Positions

1. ***What has broken free of its boundaries in my life?*** What has been born and is in need of protection? Is this a new project or plan? Is it a surprise, or something that's been expected for quite some time? How can I describe this thing to myself and others? Is it an idea, a relationship, a movement between states of being? Or is it something that, while maybe not unexpected, requires a plan to help deal with it? And let's be honest: Am I in over my head right now? It can be hard to acknowledge such a thing, but once we do, asking for help—or at least articulating to ourselves, if no one else, that we don't know what the hell we're doing—is *much* easier to do.

2. ***What do I need to watch out for that is just waiting to take advantage of my work?*** We've all got people in our lives who do this, whether they mean to or not. Even if they have the best intentions, these folks tend to pounce on new, fresh ideas, plans, or even people; and if we can help ourselves become aware that they operate this way in our lives, we can help ourselves avoid this type of person or influence.

3. ***What unstoppable force is flowing through my life that I can't control?*** Sometimes the answer to this question is obvious and even universal; for example, during the height of the Covid-19 pandemic, an out-of-control virus was clearly an unstoppable force in all our lives. But

sometimes the answer is much more subtle and personal. Maybe it's the love of a parent or the need for a steady income, or maybe it's an unhealthy behavior that we can't get out in front of.

4. ***What help do I have in shielding and protecting these new projects and plans?*** If you're anything like me, you tend to forget that help is available. I'd make the world's worst MacGyver, because once something went wrong I would just stand there screaming until a better idea occurred to me. But let's assume that's not the best way to solve a problem. Let's take as a given that help is available, and all we need to do is look around for assistance and solutions. How can we step back from our initial panic response and get ourselves into a space where others can find us and help us shield and develop these new plans that we want to get off the ground?

Sample Reading

In this spread we see Cups (Water), Wands (Fire), and a Major Arcana card that contains both, even if the Water is only implied by the varying shades of blue. There are solitary figures doing everything by themselves, and we also see groups making it happen through connection and maybe a little divine help if we're lucky. Whatever happens, we will be guided by passions, either our own or others'.

1. ***What has broken free of its boundaries in my life?*** The 9 of Cups. This card is often associated with wishes, either making them or waiting for them to come true. There's a lack of control implied here, and it's important for us to get our worms back under control quickly, because the greedy robins and scrub jays are lining up and waiting to devour our future happiness.

2. *What do I need to watch out for that is just waiting to take advantage of my work?* The 9 of Wands represents a very hard worker who has been through the wringer, who might perceive their good fortune but see it as a burden, not a joy. We're not seeing the opportunities available to handle the situation more successfully by trying something else.

3. *What unstoppable force is flowing through my life that I can't control?* The 4 of Wands shows a couple soaring between four upright wands, balancing and floating, dressed in black and white like a bride and groom on their wedding day. There's no telling if the wave they (and we) ride will be constantly on the upswell or if we're headed for a catastrophic downturn. But we get to decide if we want to be conscious as we ride the wave, even if we don't know where it's leading or whether the next swell will leave us up or down.

4. *What help do I have in shielding and protecting these new projects and plans?* The Lovers. Help is not only available, there's practically a volcano of help ready to explode in this card. An angel is literally rising to rush to our aid. Whatever issue is confronting us as we experience the March Full Worm Moon, we do not have to confront it alone.

MARCH DARK MOON

Keywords

Excess, turbulence, drama

Questions to Ponder

Consider the following as you shuffle your deck. Sometimes when dealing with fear, the best way to identify it is to ask who or what it is. What are we so afraid of right now, and why? What is this elemental energy that's blocking every move forward? What can we do to help ourselves? Who can we call on for assistance, and who or what should we avoid? Is this block larger than us? Is it ancestral and something that we need to ask for assistance in working through? What is the worst that can happen, and are we catastrophizing? If you're looking to do any ancestor work that deals with resolving lineage debt, reach out to your guides and guardians to shield and protect you as you do so.[5]

Spread

After shuffling, draw six cards and lay them out according to the following diagram.

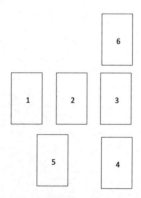

---

5 "Ancestor work" refers to engaging in processes in which we connect to our ancestors through meditation, trance, and journeywork. "Lineage debt" is the idea of debt accumulated in the past by our ancestors that is carried by the living until paid off via charitable works, personal development, or other appropriate means.

Positions

1. *What fear is most driving me right now?* If I had to name it, what would I call it? Is it an old fear or something new? Is it people-based or something to do with objects or items in my space? What words would I use to describe it? Is it big or small, all-encompassing or a wee thing I wouldn't even notice unless I went looking for it? Is it obvious or subtle? And is it something that affects just me, or am I looking at a lineage thing? This is important to take note of, because if the entire lineage is haunted by the same fear, processing it by yourself is a start, but not the whole work. Take the time to figure out what you're dealing with.

2. *How is this fear holding me back? What is the literal and figurative damage that we're looking at here?* Sometimes it's easy to ignore consequences because they're silent or invisible, but it's important to not forget that they're happening regardless of what we pretend. Once you see what the fear is, determining its effects on your life is crucial. So look with a very careful eye at how the fear you've identified is operating in your life right now.

3. *What steps can I take toward releasing my fear?* This is the "action items" portion of our program. What is your homework? What do you actually need to do about what you've discovered? Maybe others will be involved or maybe this is a solo project, but either way, definitive steps forward are required to move things along.

4. *Who or what are my allies during this process?* Who can help you, or at the very least, who can you rely on to bounce things off of without spilling your secrets all over the internet? This card can also indicate who to listen to when it comes to advice; pay attention here, because

not everybody is able to offer the best or most pertinent advice, no matter how much they want to or how hard they try.

5. *Who or what are my enemies during this process? Who or what should be avoided as this process unfolds?* This doesn't mean that people are evil or have bad intent, although maybe they do. But perhaps it's best to avoid well-intentioned people who just don't understand what you're going through or how important the process is to you. Only you will know best how to deal with these people, but take note of what comes up so that you can see what kind of boundaries you need to create. You might need to do something as small as turning off your electronic devices for an hour or two a day, or as big as practicing saying "no" to everybody and everything for a while.

6. *What is the wind that will take away the emotional and energetic baggage and dissolve it? What can help get rid of the leftovers?* Once you've identified the shadow, worked with it to find out what it's about, and done the work to move past it, is there cleanup left to do? Any closure needed? If so, what will help you ritualize and make real the step of letting go and moving on?

Sample Reading

Notice right away that there are two Aces in this draw, signifying elemental beginnings in the realms of Earth (Pentacles) and Fire (Wands). We are dealing with beginnings, or rather, we're dealing with an old problem in new ways. We've got one Major Arcana card, the Devil himself, and we've got two court cards (the Knight of Pentacles and the Queen of Cups). Looking at the cards as a set, we can see that there's a lot of openness and flowing energy, both within each card and between them. The only darkness is around the Devil; everything else is open and clear in a "what you see is what you get" kind of way. Yet it's worth noting that the light flows around the darkness in the center without ever penetrating it. The core issue is untouched by the energies all around it.

1. *What fear is most driving me right now?* The 10 of Cups. All the energy in this card could be overwhelming to someone who is used to keeping their emotions bottled up. It's not only happiness that's the main fear here; it's also that since this is the 10, there's nowhere to go but down.

2. *How is this fear holding me back?* The Devil. I don't see this card as representative of any particular evil personage, but rather as a representation of my own fears that get projected outward, magnified, and mirrored back to me—usually as unhealthy behaviors, limiting patterns, or even addictions. If we stopped looking at the future through fear goggles, would we see possibility?

3. *What steps can I take toward releasing my fear?* The Ace of Wands. Move beyond the realm of the emotional self and into the realm of fire, passion, and drive. Stop focusing on how everything feels and start focusing on activities, action steps, and to-do lists. Get organized!

4. *Who or what are my allies during this process?* The Queen of Cups. Our best allies are those who love us and know and care what we're going through. These are folks who know how to navigate the treacherous waters of the heart and can advise and guide us as we try to sort out how to get past the Devil there.

5. *Who or what are my enemies during this process?* The Knight of Pentacles. This is a card of creature comforts in the Tarot, the "Knight Who Loves Snacks and Naps." But when facing challenging tasks, don't become one

with the couch. Get up. Move around. Stretch. Then ask yourself the hard question you've been avoiding.

6. *What is the wind that will take away the emotional and energetic baggage and dissolve it?* The Ace of Pentacles is a card about taking that project we thought about earlier and doing the step-by-step work to make it happen. We have to take the necessary steps to get where we want to go.

Spring Equinox

Keywords

Balance, renewal, beginnings, birth

When I was growing up, Easter celebrations meant chocolate candies, pastel colors, baby everythings, family dinners, and lots of church. Weeks of it, in fact: going to Mass during the schooldays leading up to Easter weekend, spending most of Good Friday in church, then going to Mass again on Easter Sunday to honor the resurrection. It was very much about that one day, or rather that one set of three days, Easter weekend. Once it had passed, the spiritual process had been completed and we were back to our daily lives on Easter Monday—although those first few days after Easter did include a lot more candy than usual, until my siblings and I polished off every scrap.

When I was older, I began to practice a more earth-honoring spiritual path that marked the Vernal Equinox rather than the Christian resurrection. I noticed that the festival of Ostara, a non-Christian holiday that takes place at around this time, wasn't so much about commemorating a single moment or event in time, but rather marking a larger shift between the way things were and the way they were becoming. The earth was warming up. California's winter landscape of rolling hills shifted over the course of a few weeks: from a sparse, empty gray to soft green for a month or so before drying out into the warm, grassy gold it is famous for, which would last the rest of the year until the rains came again. The black-tailed deer near my home started showing up with their wobbly, spotted babies, and young squirrels raced everywhere—up and down trees, across telephone wires—making a huge hollering racket as they sorted out territory and other squirrel business. Once I started paying attention to what was going on all around me, using all my senses and not just my mind, it was obvious that the time of light had begun and the time of dark was fading. The great cosmic Wheel had turned another notch, and all the growing things were awake and clamoring to be seen by the sun.

Given the momentous shift in energies that happens on a quarter day, it's a perfect time to explore how best to use the changing energy to identify and release old patterns that aren't working for us, and to begin new practices that will help us get to where we want to be. This is true for any of the solstices or equinoxes, so what makes Ostara different? It's the time of beginnings, of births and newness. It's also a reminder, for formerly agrarian societies that lived very close to the land, to start planting. So when Ostara comes around, we can start thinking about how to begin working toward any resolutions for the year that we haven't started on yet, and we can also think about how to deepen those actions that we've already begun. Taking inspiration from all the literal baby steps happening around us, we can break down our great big goals into little actions that might be clumsy and unglamorous but, when taken together, create progress that we didn't think was possible.

Questions to Ponder
Consider the following as you shuffle your deck. What seeds can we plant at this time? And, perhaps more specifically, what do we want to harvest later in the year that we must start planning for now? How can we begin to add fresh beauty into our lives after a long winter? Do we want the winds of change to do a gentle shuffling of our energies, or do we want a complete clearing of the decks?

Southern Hemisphere
If it's useful for you, please feel free to switch the spreads and read about the Spring Equinox in September and the Autumnal Equinox in March.

As the Wheel turns and directs you toward the colder, darker months, preparation is always a good idea. How can you begin to gather up what you'll need as you enter a time of withdrawal and potential lack? Is there any big project you've been putting off because it seems impossible, that maybe you can break down into smaller and smaller steps so that it becomes not only manageable but a source of pride and energy?

Spread

After shuffling, draw six cards and lay them out according to the following diagram.

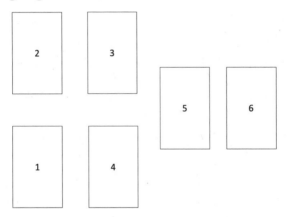

Positions

1. *What can be left behind in the dark?* What is the shell we've been growing in, the cocoon that has been nourishing us and that we now need to break free from and leave behind? It's tempting to stay buried, but life is a forward-pushing process, and we cannot allow ourselves to stay stuck. Like little turtles or birds, we have to break free from the containers we have been growing within because, at the very least, we no longer fit inside them. As we grow, we need room. And like the bear emerging from

hibernation, we're probably hungry for nourishment to feed our newly minted selves.

2. *What needs to come out into the sun?* What is the truth coming forth? What is being born at this moment? It may be a new self entirely, or it might be something small and hardly noticeable to anyone but you. Is it possible that something is emerging and even you don't know what it is? Yes, of course that's absolutely possible. Anybody who's gone through puberty (or menopause!) can tell you that's true. Take a look at what's emerging as if you've never seen or thought about it before, so that you don't miss facets of it that might be important to know later.

3. *How can I best protect and shelter the precious new thing?* Do I need to send out a "birth announcement"? Or do I keep my mouth shut and not tell anybody about what's going on with me? Maybe my way forward is somewhere in between. But in any case, the new thing needs protection. If it's a change we've been working on for a while, maybe we don't have to announce it to the world just yet. Or maybe we only share our new change with a small group of trusted friends and advisers. Perhaps we don't tell anyone until we feel more secure in what's at stake. In any case, it's useful to know in advance what kind of protection is needed and what might be overkill.

4. *What ideas can be planted like seeds for harvest later in the year?* Take a good look six months into the future. Where do you want to be, both with your new precious thing and with your life in general? There are obviously life events that can't be planned for or built around, but those are going to happen whatever we do, so let's leave them aside for now. Where do you want to be in six months? What do you want to be working on

or manifesting? Those are the seeds we can plant now so that they'll be ready to emerge at the next equinox.

5. *How can I tap into the energy of the equinox to bring more balance into my life?* The passage of the year is broken into segments to help us mark our paths as we go. The equinoxes are good times to check in with ourselves regarding where we're spending our time and energy. Is it in balance or not? If not, where do we need to back off a bit, and where can we lean forward and put some energy in, to bring the balance back?

6. *What special surprises await me as the Great Wheel turns today?* With a nod toward all the egg hunts and spring baskets full of candy and presents, let's ask for a surprise for ourselves on this holiday! And once you receive your present from the cosmos, how can you share it or make the best use of it, for the benefit of all beings?

Sample Reading

Considering Ostara or the Vernal Equinox as a quarter day and a point of balance, it makes sense that there are both Major and Minor Arcana cards in this draw: the two Major Arcana cards are on a diagonal to one another, creating a balancing point between the endings represented by Death and the acceptance and incorporation of those endings, and the new truths created from them, represented by Temperance. We also see an Ace next to the Death card—endings and beginnings together—and the giving and receiving qualities of both the 6 of Pentacles and the Temperance card. Taking all this together, the reading shows us cards of beginnings and cards of endings, cards of small matters and cards of great power. Let the theme of balance direct how you see your cards when you lay them out. Who and what do you see? What suits are present? What numbers, colors, shapes, and figures?

1. *What can be left behind in the dark?* The 6 of Pentacles. A figure gives coins to other figures who look like they could use some help. In the context of this draw, perhaps what needs to be left behind is the constant giving.

2. *What needs to come out into the sun?* Death. It's a startling image to see in any reading, let alone an Ostara reading, that's for sure. But the message here is plain and simple: it's time to deal with endings. We are born, we live, and we die, and as we age we need to start preparing for our exit.

3. *How can I best protect and shelter the precious new thing?* The Ace of Wands. Time to make an estate plan, people! It may be strange and difficult to think about wills and advance directives while everything else around you is about bright colors and sunlight, but taking a few small steps every day in planning and preparing will leave time to enjoy the blossoming of life while respecting the eventuality of death.

4. *What ideas can be planted like seeds for harvest later in the year?* Temperance is about balance and alchemy, about the process that happens to the caterpillar once it cocoons itself in order to become a butterfly. Right now is the time to plant the seeds of change. Right now is the time to start preparing for whatever is to come and to allow it to happen.

5. *How can I tap into the energy of the equinox to bring more balance into my life?* The 2 of Cups. Often considered the "marriage" card, in this context it's more like the "get help" card, which will bring the balance back; because as we saw in the first card, the 6 of Pentacles, we've been trying to do it all alone without success. Here in the 2 of Cups we see two figures presenting their cups

as equals. That's a symbol of balance that we need to practice going forward.

6. *What special surprises await me as the Great Wheel turns today?* The Queen of Pentacles is the queen of the good home, the warm and comforting Lady of the Manor who loves and cares for all within her domain. Let yourself be helped by her: she has plenty to share and more than enough for everyone.

April

THE FULL MOON

*A*pril in the Northern Hemisphere tends to bring sunlight, heat, and the possibilities of life outdoors into our lives in earnest. Depending on where you live, it could also bring wind, humidity, and rain. Where I live in the San Francisco Bay Area, April provides a sort of pause between our two-season reality of wind and fire versus rain and fog; it's a view of what growing seasons used to be before the earth let us know what the consequences of two centuries of increasing fossil-fuel dependence really look like out here. There might be a short heat wave in April, which is a joy to every student heading out for spring break. There might be a passing storm or two, reminding travelers that nature is not to be taken for granted no matter what the weather was like at dawn. There's a sort of delighted chaotic quality to April's energy that might have something to do with getting our taxes completed and filed by April 15—if you live and work in the US, that is; and even if not, there's a sense that the Wheel has turned and we're moving toward summer. Even if summer is not our favorite season, it's still a season of getting things done, of activity and accomplishment and movement, which, as members of the human community, we gravitate toward with energy and anticipation.

The full moon in April is sometimes called the "Pink Moon" because of the riot of flowers that appear in all of nature's mad, glorious colors. Roses, poppies, daisies, irises, lilies, and wildflowers of a thousand different kinds emerge, and with them (hopefully for millennia to come) the bees doing their essential work of pollination and expansion. Nature is at work, and the call is out for us to join her.

The Full Moon—Southern Hemisphere

Where is beauty in the natural world around you? Even if things look dim, dull, or dying, there is still beauty. Do you appreciate it? Can you see other beings working hard to get ready for winter, like the squirrels, insects, birds, or other small animals of your landscape? Are you able to find joy in your work, even if the bustle feels a bit more like a desperate hustle than might be comfortable for you? Let the wide-ranging joyful energy of this moon fill you up and help you prepare for the leaner months to come.

THE DARK MOON

When April's dark moon rolls around, we have an opportunity to look closely at how we're managing our relationships with community. We've moved out of the sheltering phase of winter in the Northern Hemisphere and may now be actively participating in communal engagements. There are spring vacations, school dances, social and spiritual activities with our various communities, and all manner of opportunities to reengage with others. But while we might be used to thinking of ourselves as the heroes of our own stories, it can be beneficial to take the opportunity presented by the shadow of the Pink Moon to look at where our "hero" self-image might actually be more accurately characterized as "tyrant" or "martyr."

These aren't complimentary ways to see ourselves, but it can be useful to try to see how we show up this way so that we can learn where our weaknesses are and maybe make better choices—or at least more honest choices—in our interactions with others. There's a moment in the movie *The First Wives Club* where, during an argument, Diane Keaton's character proclaims, "But I'm the nice one!" and the other two first wives laugh uproariously at her because they know she's not really nice. She's a resentful pushover, a bitter victim who uses her long-suffering image to manipulate those around her to get what she wants. This was difficult for this character to hear, but once she had heard it, she was able to face this truth about herself and become more honest in her communications going forward. So how can we apply these lessons to ourselves—without aggression or attack, but instead with compassion and a desire for thoughtful change?

The Dark Moon—Southern Hemisphere

This dark moon presents a perfect opportunity to review how we perceive ourselves in relation to others and to take a closer and more discerning look at where we let ourselves off the hook. Perhaps since the light is fading in the Southern Hemisphere, it's a perfect time to pick up this challenge as something that can be worked on throughout the winter.

APRIL FULL MOON

Keywords
Chaos, warmth, growth, energy

Questions to Ponder
Consider the following as you shuffle your deck. Where is our joy, especially in work? What is around us that makes us happy? How do we reward ourselves for completing responsibilities? Do we allow ourselves to take breaks, even small ones, or are we all work all the time? Do we acknowledge and celebrate the variety of beauty all around us?

When we think about getting down to business, about doing the work of our lives, whatever that might be, do we do so joyfully or with dread? Is it a thing we *get* to do or a thing we *have* to do? Let this month's full moon be a good time for you to reconsider how you work and what energy you bring to getting it done.

Spread

After shuffling, draw five cards and lay them out according to the following diagram.

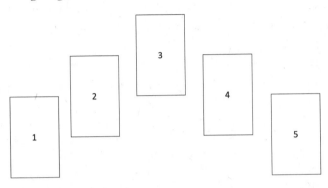

Positions

1. *How can I be more like the bees?* In what way can I focus more on the work I need to be doing, seeing it not as a burden, but as a non-emotional process in which I must engage as a fellow human being on this planet? We can assign emotions to our bee friends as they work: busy, friendly, happy, etc. But if we remove that and just watch what they're doing, what do we see? They do the work. That's it. They are driven by their own bee nature to go from plant to plant collecting what the hive needs to survive. We don't know if they hate their job or love it or what they feel; all we know is that each day they do their work to accomplish the group goal so that all can thrive.

2. *What beauty and magic are in my life right now that I'm not seeing?* This is another way of asking where our focus is and how we can shift it. What are we seeing, and what are we missing if we have blinders on? Or are we so focused on one way of seeing, one view or landscape that we're used to, that we miss important details that

we might have seen if we'd only looked around a bit? Another point of this question is to discover what magic is present in everyday "ordinary" things. If we take it as a given that magic is everywhere, all we have to do is see it to begin the process of making use of it. So how do we see it? How do we recognize it?

3. ***How can I bring more joy into my work?*** What can I do or stop doing to let joyful energy in, or to create joyful energy if I'm currently stuck or feel like I'm stagnating? Joy isn't the only energy for change. I recently got a fortune from a fortune cookie that told me despair is an agent for change, and after staring at the fortune for a minute and reeling from the audacity of this flimsiest of cookies, I could see the truth behind it. But joy is a powerful energy for change too, and it's more fun to work with in my opinion.

4. ***What do I need to let go of that's bringing me down?*** Joy is a light energy, not a heavy one. It's frothy, airy, and unattached. Have you ever laughed for no reason? Maybe you and a friend got on a tear about something and pretty soon you were cracking each other up just by looking at one another? That's the energy of joy at work, and it has to work too hard if it's weighed down by cares, worries, regret, guilt, or shame—so let some of that go. What's ready to be released?

5. ***How can I reward myself right now?*** What little treat or escape would be best for you to take? Where does spring break fit into your plans? If you can't afford to get away physically, can you take a mental break? Have you developed habits that could use a reset? What can you do in the material world that will help you manifest a reality shift, which is all a vacation really is? And another thing: Have you accomplished something that you haven't given

yourself credit for? Use this time to take that credit. You deserve it.

Sample Reading

When we take an overall look at the spread, we see four cards with solitary figures and a fifth card with multiple masked figures moving away from one another. There's something to keep in mind as we go: What are we turning away from, and what do we need to turn our backs on? There is one Major Arcana card and four Minor Arcana cards, indicating that the energy is mostly grounded in our day-to-day lives and is only specifically tapping into the powerful energy of the whole human flow. There is focus in these cards as well: the individual figures are each immersed in their own environment and situation, and by contemplating them we're invited to focus just as intently on where we are and what we're doing.

1. *How can I be more like the bees?* The 10 of Swords. What we need to do is focus on the work in front of us and stop worrying about what we can't do anything about. Another way of looking at it would be to make a brainstorm diagram in which you write down everything you're worried about, then delete anything you can't control. You've thought about it as much as you can. More thinking won't help.

2. *What beauty and magic are in my life right now that I'm not seeing?* The 5 of Cups. We are focused so profoundly on what we've lost that we completely miss what remains. In order to focus on the magic and beauty in our lives this April, the instruction is to turn our backs on the past and take stock of what we have left. It's where the beauty and magic are.

3. *How can I bring more joy into my work?* The Hanged Man tells us to take a pause, to chill out and await further instructions. More joy (or perhaps peace) can be achieved by ceasing all effort to create joy and by just being in whatever environment we're in.

4. *What do I need to let go of that's bringing me down?* The 9 of Wands in this context is a card of having had to be strong for too long. It's another card in this spread that's advising us to let go of needing to manage everything and to practice just being in the moment we're in.

5. *How can I reward myself right now?* The 6 of Swords is a card of escape and release, so it's perfect in the position that reflects what we can do to treat ourselves. How can you take a vacation from how you're used to thinking about things and give yourself a new perspective?

APRIL DARK MOON

Keywords
Martyrdom, resentment, escapism, retreat

Questions to Ponder
Consider the following as you shuffle your deck. How do we show up for work, both physically and metaphorically? In this post-Covid era of hybrid workspaces and Zoom calls, do we slough off more than just the formalities we used to accept without thinking? Do we let ourselves get drained by all this electronic contact, where there used to be constant in-person connection or phone calls? Have we let laziness about who we are and what we're capable of take over, because it's easier to keep doing things the same old way than to explore new, more honest and deliberate ways of releasing our limiting and hurtful self-perception?

How do we show up? Are we the same when no one else is around as we are in front of a crowd? There are different levels of authenticity that we apply to different situations. The idea isn't to be searingly honest with everyone at all times, because such honesty might not be appropriate. But we can—and must—always be honest with ourselves.

Spread
After shuffling, draw four cards and lay them out according to the following diagram.

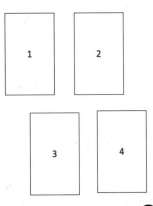

Positions

1. *Where am I on the authenticity scale?* This is a way of asking ourselves whether we spend most of our time coming from a place of authentic communication or from a more hidden and duplicitous place. It's worth it to try to avoid judgment here. There may be perfectly good reasons for inauthenticity at times—if we are in unsafe or toxic environments and relationships, for example. If we are surrounded by people who manipulate honest communications for their own ends, it makes sense to keep masks in place. But do we wear those masks when we don't need to—when perhaps we would really benefit from being more authentic to ourselves?

2. *Why am I at that level of either visibility or duplicity?* This card provides a deeper look into the previous question so that we can explore why we wear the masks. What is the cause of our behavior, and is there anything about it that we can change for the better? Are there elements we can release? Is there a long-term process at work that we can take a look at and see if it's time to remove some of its power?

3. *What do I need most to help me stay authentic to my actual needs?* Whatever the reason for why we are how we are right now, what can help us achieve greater authenticity in our communications? What can help us be more direct, more honest, at the very least with ourselves? What tools do we have or can we acquire that will assist us in this work?

4. *Where are my blind spots on this issue?* What am I not seeing that could help or hurt me?

Sample Reading

An overview of these cards shows us three Minors and a Major Arcana card, two cards of multiple figures and two cards of solitary figures, an awful lot of brightness and yellow, and a little bit of darkness that seems to swamp everything around it. The cards show both giving and suffering, and a sort of holding space that is filled with either riches or smugness. Each card has some element of blue in it, indicating the presence of an important emotional state, and there are no Swords (Air) or Wands (Fire) in this draw but only Cups (Water) and Pentacles (Earth). Air or Fire would indicate thoughts and thinking, which leads me to surmise that our authentic self is somehow rooted in how we manifest our emotions.

1. *Where am I on the authenticity scale?* The 6 of Pentacles. Finding our way clear to seeing our position honestly and without judgment is key to authentic communication with others, because it helps us see what our needs actually are. Balance and justice in manifestation is a good goal to keep in sight.

2. *Why am I at that level of either visibility or duplicity?* The Hanged Man. Western culture is rooted in Christianity-based transactionalism that divides actions and perceptions into binaries like good versus evil and happy versus sad, which will send us to heaven or hell when we die. What's motivating our transactions? Now is not the time for action, but for considering this and its effects on our behavior while the dust settles.

3. *What do I need most to help me stay authentic to my actual needs?* The 9 of Cups is a card about getting real with what you really want. If we want to get a new job, we have to explore those resources and familiarize ourselves with what new jobs are available. If we want a

new relationship, we have to start looking for it. Dig out the details of what you want. Get specific.

4. ***Where are my blind spots on this issue?*** The 5 of Pentacles. "Poverty consciousness" is another thing that Western society has given us: the belief that either we are not good enough or what we receive is not good enough, or maybe both. What thoughts about self-worth can be shifted so that we can perceive what we think we're missing? What are we taking for granted?

Bealtaine

Keywords
Beauty, sex, fertility, passionate energy

With the exception of Samhain, Bealtaine is likely the most widely known of all the holidays in the witch's year. If you've heard the song "The Lusty Month of May" from the musical *Camelot*, you've got a sense of what Bealtaine is about: life. Glorious, messy, beautiful, sexy, energetic, chaotic, joyful life. And it marks the point on the Wheel directly opposite from Samhain. Both are fire festivals, but the May Eve celebration of Bealtaine, which is Irish for "month of May," is a celebration of all the good, fun things in life that build our sense of self, community, and how we live and work together. Like Samhain, its origins in Ireland are very old and rooted in agrarian activities and lifestyles that no longer drive most of us in our daily lives, but Bealtaine continues to captivate practitioners of European-based earth-honoring faiths that track the movements of both sun and moon throughout the year. We may not all plow the earth or plant crops or know what it means to worry that a hailstorm or insect infestation will lead to community starvation, but as the climate emergency takes hold in our modern world, we very much know what it means to be afraid of wildfires, floods, pandemics, or monster storms fueled by warming seas. The precariousness of life makes us all the more aware of how precious it is, so taking opportunities to celebrate the joy of being alive is as old as humankind.

Fertility is a big theme in Bealtaine celebrations as well, and while the sexual element from the festival's origins remains, those who don't want or enjoy sexual experiences also have ways and reasons to celebrate today. For those who do enjoy sex and/ or want to procreate, there's room for that too. Honoring the combination of divine energies in the creation of new life is also as old as being human and will always represent hope, the future, and another chance that with faith, right action, and good work, we as a community can be better than we were before.

Questions to Ponder

Consider the following as you shuffle your deck. What do we have to celebrate right now? Where can we find joy? What is getting in the way of our creative expressions, whatever those might be? What do we want to give birth to at this time, and what do we need to do to make that happen? If times are hard (and they are, for many of us), what can we do to help ourselves find joy? How can we help others find their joy too? What do we want to create at this time? What energies do we want to work with to bring our dreams into reality? Get clear on what you're asking for. Shake off the heaviness, the cobwebs, and any fear you're sitting with and reach out for joy, for pleasure, and for goodness. Now is the time to dance, however that might look for you. Sing! Clap! Move around in whatever way you like best.

Southern Hemisphere

The veils between realities are very thin right now, no matter what side of the world you live on. If you are not experiencing Bealtaine you are experiencing Samhain, and both are times for checking in with your ancestors and spirit guides and asking for any guidance you need. Bealtaine celebrations are about life and Samhain observances are about death, but your beloved dead will always have thoughts and ideas to share about how to live your best life.

Spread

After shuffling, draw eight cards and lay them out according to the following diagram.

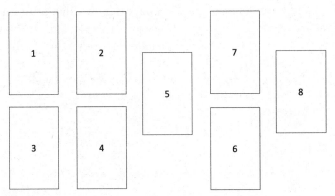

Positions

1. *What do I want to give birth to right now?* This might actually be better explained as "what do I *need* to give birth to right now?" If we already know what we want, that's great and it helps tremendously when doing manifestation magic. The question then becomes, What do we need to do in order to manifest our desires? We can turn our focus to that and work on it from that angle. But if we aren't yet clear on what we want, asking for assistance doesn't hurt. Sometimes we're caught between two or more ideas that we can't choose between, and it can be useful to let the cards provide a cardboard assist. Also, there are folks who have never gotten into the practice of formulating and manifesting their desires, so starting with a "what I want to create" baseline is a good idea for them.

2. *Who can I connect with to bring my project to life?* Who are my helpers, my allies? This is also a good position for the relationship or lover question. If you are looking for a companion or partner, be sure to consider whether or not they will be compatible with your goals, and whether you are compatible with theirs. Sometimes we find partners so

that we don't have to be alone, or so that we can have some fun, and that's great. Nothing wrong there. But in this particular case, we're looking for connection and joyful project sharing. Think, for instance, of having a baby. That's a project, right? And if so, you want to "work" on that with someone you love, a partner you can share the joys and sorrows of parenthood with for the long term. You want to find someone who will be in it with you for the long haul.

3. *What energies can I tap into to help me celebrate?* The answer to this particular question might seem obvious, but I don't think it is. Think of a casino. The energy there can be very celebratory, but it can also be vampiric. There is so much need, such a feeling of being trapped, that an innocent wandering in will be devoured in an instant. So we need to be careful when we talk about the energy we want to bring up and connect to as we celebrate all the goodness in our lives. This question can also be challenging for folks who are suffering losses and who maybe could use a little help in finding reasons to be happy. This isn't about negating grief or anger or any other manifestation of suffering in any way; instead, it's about bringing joy and gratitude onto the scene in whatever authentic way works for us in the moment.

4. *What can I bring to community at this time (that is, what do I bring to the table)?* Maybe I have more than others right now, or maybe I have a skill that can help— maybe I make the best mashed potatoes on the planet, or the best mead, or maybe I play a mean guitar or sing with all my heart. All these gifts help us connect with one another as a group. Sometimes we help by giving to charity, and sometimes our gifts are less material and more intangible; either way, giving matters.

5. *What is blocking me from sharing my joy?* Are we letting current worries get in the way of celebration and joyful expression? It's easy to do, especially when we're in the middle of hard times. So what do we need to get out of the way? What needs to get put down for a little while so that we can get our groove back?

6. *What words of wisdom do my ancestors have for me now?* This card will allow the ancestors to speak. If you don't have an active ancestor practice, never fear. The messages will still come. And if you do have an ancestor practice, this message will be from the ones who are healed and whole and can bring you wisdom that will be of most service to you and your lineages.

7. *What message does my Higher Self or Deity of Choice have to carry me through until Samhain?* If you work with a particular deity or deities, this card will offer them the opportunity to speak should they wish to at this time (we are very polite with them and do not make demands but only ask for a message and always say "please"). You will know if they are responding. Otherwise, this card will be a message to you from your Higher Self about how this Bealtaine can provide you with the opportunities you need to bring your creative dreams to life.

8. *Because this is a Big Energy Day, let's draw a wild card to show us what an overview of the next six months will be.* For those who are new to the cards, a wild card is a card that doesn't have a set position in the spread; it represents the operation of Fate in the reading. I'm a big fan of wild cards because they offer us the opportunity to peek into the great rolling Dice Cup of Fate to see what could possibly come up and change everything. Big Energy Days are a particularly good time to do this, although you can draw a wild card at any time.

Sample Reading

If we do a quick overview of the cards to see what we're working with, we've got three Major Arcana cards, five Minors, and all the suits represented except Cups (Water). Getting into Bealtaine and celebrating life billowing all around us is going to be a less emotional and more physical and mental process for us. There isn't too much drama going on except right in the middle with the Tower, but we'll get to that. Most of the cards feature single individuals, but the one Minor Arcana card with multiple figures represents the family grouping, so we can say that we're looking at how we relate to others in bringing our ability to share joy out into the world. There are also a lot of Swords present, so our mental processes are on display here.

1. *What do I want to give birth to right now?* The Ace of Swords is a card of brilliant flashes, great ideas, and that spectacular sense of knowing we get when a new idea presents itself. This card offers us the opportunity to approach Bealtaine with Bright Idea Energy that says, "Hey! I know how we can change that!" Let's bring out the new and different!

2. *Who can I connect with to bring my project to life?* The Queen of Swords is the genius of the Tarot: clear-minded, articulate, far-seeing, and about as no-nonsense as you can get. If your project is a labor of love, you will definitely want someone like the Queen of Swords to provide planning and brainstorming.

3. *What energies can I tap into to help me celebrate?* The Fool. No one knows what will happen when we take that leap of faith. In this context, we're asking what energies we can tap into to help us celebrate this Bealtaine, and the Fool is here to tell us to do it all our own brand-new way.

4. ***What can I bring to community at this time (that is, what do I bring to the table)?*** The 4 of Swords is about as far from a "party animal" card as you can get, and that's ok. What we bring to community in celebration of life is a calm, cool, relaxed presence. No judgment is passed and no arguments encouraged.

5. ***What is blocking me from sharing my joy?*** The Tower is a card of big changes that come out of nowhere and that you can't prepare for or do anything about except to just hang on and ride it out. We are asking what is blocking us from sharing our joy, and the Tower is telling us that massive global events are all in the way. Any act of creativity in this time, no matter how small, is a raised fist in honor of life itself.

6. ***What words of wisdom do my ancestors have for me now?*** The King of Wands is a master of creation, a big-idea person who brings passion and excitement to everything he does. Our ancestors are suggesting that we give our projects, plans, and creative ideas for Bealtaine and beyond a strong, well-thought-out, and well-developed structure that will support them through to completion.

7. ***What message does my Higher Self or Deity of Choice have to carry me through until Samhain?*** The 10 of Pentacles can be read as the card of the ancestors. Our Deity or Higher Self is suggesting that we listen to our ancestors and do what they suggest in the previous card. We are being reminded to keep our families in mind when we proceed with our projects and plans.

8. ***Because this is a Big Energy Day, let's draw a wild card to show us what an overview of the next six months will be.*** The Empress is about life here on Earth, and as

much as Bealtaine is a celebration of life, the Empress is a manifestation of female-presenting energy in the way we organize and live our lives. As tempting as it is to see the Empress as a kindly mother figure, though, she's called the Empress for a reason. From here to Samhain in the Northern Hemisphere, we must prepare ourselves for her to take matters into her own hands to clear the air and bring stability and peace back to all her children.

May

THE FULL MOON

*D*uring the full moon in May, everything is in flower. The expansive energy of full moons in general is given a cheery explosion of color and possibility, and if we're wise and alert we can use this energy to fuel our ideas, intentions, and plans for the rest of the year. We can tap into the energy of beauty, resilience, and changeability to bring vitality to our creations and joy to our celebrations this month. The possibility exists for a more profound understanding of how we function in the community and where we can better serve others by deepening our commitment to each other.

May can be a time of bright, brilliant color, warmth, passionate energy, and new possibilities all around. In many places the school year is ending, and summer vacation is like a light at the end of a long tunnel for students who have been studying hard for months. It can also be a good time to start looking with intention at what you want to create, what you have already created since the beginning of the year, and what has absolutely taken over with chaotic abandon that might need to be pruned back to make room for what's to come.

In the US we also celebrate a holiday we call "Memorial Day" in May. It's a day we set aside to honor those who have died while serving in our military. We remember their sacrifice and look to our own blessings with gratitude. We also celebrate the unofficial beginning of summer at the same time, thereby allowing the energy of May to move us forward in the year with both solemnity and a joyful connection to life itself.

The Full Moon—Southern Hemisphere

As you approach your winter or rainy season, looking for beauty and joy in the world around you couldn't be more valuable. Finding ways to bring those elements into your life with creativity and celebration will provide a source of comfort and hope in the days to come.

THE DARK MOON

As much as May is a time of celebration and remembrance, the dark moon of May is a useful time to take a hard look at how we overdo it, where our energies let us down, and where we let ourselves get away with all kinds of nonsense for all kinds of reasons. Do we engage in unhealthy behavior? Or maybe we pour so much of ourselves into celebrations for others that we completely (perhaps deliberately) forget how much we ourselves need replenishment, and so we push on in bitterness and unacknowledged anger. Let's use this dark moon time to turn inward and get real with ourselves about where community celebration becomes just another reason to overindulge in whatever our poison of choice happens to be.

Do brides ever start out trying to be a "bridezilla"? Does anyone who is getting married begin their journey thinking, "I'm going to get so swept away by this already overwhelming process that I am going to gleefully treat everyone around me like garbage and I'm going to love every minute of it"? Of course not. It's an example of letting the shadow side of a person's energy take over and run the whole show without ever getting reined in by the common-sense side. Or maybe you're a workaholic, or someone who is addicted to perfection. What is going on behind the noise?

The Dark Moon—Southern Hemisphere

Though autumn is in full swing for you rather than spring, the very big energies of the recent fire festival of Samhain are still likely causing vibrations far and wide across your reality. How are the shadows of Samhain reflected in this dark moon? Are your ancestors and other beloved dead still speaking loudly, and do they have anything to share about how you can work with the shadows that flow through your lineages and that may show up as personal self-management difficulties? Can they help you face what needs to be faced right now?

MAY FULL MOON
Keywords
Life, resilience, passion, adaptability

Questions to Ponder
Consider the following questions as you shuffle your deck. How and where do we notice and celebrate the beauty all around us? How can we honor those who went before and gave their lives so that we can live and flourish and thrive now? What is ending in our lives, or what needs to end so that other things can begin? How can we mark the shifting time with joy, and how can we best release regret and suffering so that we don't carry it forward with us? And since honoring motherhood in all its forms happens during May in many places, it is worthwhile to ask ourselves how we honor and experience motherhood, whether we have offspring or not. How do we show up as mothers in our own lives, and how do we nurture ourselves when we need it most?

Spread
After shuffling, draw five cards and lay them out according to the following diagram.

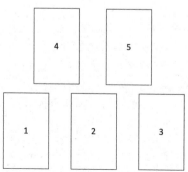

Positions

1. *What do I need to honor in my life that I'm currently not seeing?* Sometimes we need to recognize and honor a passage of life or an event, and it just doesn't occur to us to do it because we're busy. No judgment—we're in the middle of hard and challenging times, so finding ways to honor things seems like a luxury we may not have time for. But we're being called to make time. We need to look around and see what is passing or what's already passed, either in ourselves or in the world around us. We're experiencing so much change that marking passages is a great way to help ourselves remember and process where we've been and what's happened in our lives.

2. *How can I add to the joy of life for my community and myself?* Here's another element that's even more critical the harder things get. Alice Walker said, "Hard times require furious dancing," and the organization Radical Joy for Hard Times is all about this. How do we add to the goodness of the world around us rather than adding to the wounding? How can we leave a place, our place, our community, better than we found it? This is a hard question because resources for many people are getting slimmer and slimmer these days, but it's a good challenge to think of beauty and joy without regard to financial resources. Before everybody had money, how did we celebrate things? What do we have to share that can help bring ease and comfort to shattered communities?

3. *What weeding and pruning do I need to do in my life?* Some of us really need help with this one, so it's valuable to ask what we can let go of or prune back in our lives. Sometimes things take more energy than we realize, so put some thought into what you can realistically cut back on to make room for what's really important. Make sure

you have the energy to spend on the critical things instead of being completely worn out by things that don't matter.

4. ***How can I bring more organization to the chaos in my life?*** If you think of your life as a garden, what's taking over? What is getting completely out of hand and could use some time under the weed whacker? A Facebook acquaintance of mine posted yesterday that she's got two trees' worth of crabapples that she doesn't have the time or energy to do anything with, so she put out the call to our common acquaintances to see if anybody wanted to make buckets of crabapple jam or if she should try to donate them to a food bank. That's the kind of effort we're looking at here. Where are we buried under crabapples that we aren't planning on doing anything with, and what can we do to get rid of them usefully so we can put our energy where we want it to go?

5. ***What beauty is already around me that I'm missing?*** Given that so much of life has become unpleasant, difficult, and hair-raising, it helps to look around once in a while and really *see* beauty. I'm reminded of Tupac Shakur, the beloved award-winning rapper who wrote a poem called "The Rose That Grew from Concrete." The brilliant poet came from desperate circumstances and became one of the greatest of his generation when no one expected him to. Who saw his beauty before he became famous? Can we look around and see past our blinders, our biases, and our filters to what is really all around us? What are we missing?

Sample Reading

In looking at our cards, if we take a moment to notice what sort of general themes and symbols appear, the first thing we might see is the color present in the cards. There's red, gold, blue, and green, and it's valuable to notice what, if anything, those colors mean to you. Red can be a color of great passion and fire, and it's interesting to note that every suit except Wands (Fire) is represented here. It's possible, therefore, that the red color is picking up the energetic slack created by the absence of Wands. We see Cups, Pentacles, and Swords, and we have a Major Arcana card as well, which indicates big themes running through our reading. There are also two Aces, indicating the spark of initiation and beginnings.

1. *What do I need to honor in my life that I'm currently not seeing?* The 3 of Swords, a card of heart-wounding or betrayal of the heart by the head. What hurt have we sustained, or what loss have we suffered, that we either are ignoring or haven't thoroughly grieved? Take the time to mourn and feel the loss.

2. *How can I add to the joy of life for my community and myself?* The Hierophant tells us clearly: Lead. Get out and help people. Don't wait to be asked (although always remember to ask for consent); find ways to be the leader you are.

3. *What weeding and pruning do I need to do in my life?* The Ace of Swords is the Big Idea, and it's a sword for a reason: you can direct energy with it, but you can also cut with it. Cut those ties that are damaging to your psyche. Cut away the critical voices you've been carrying all your life that say you aren't good enough.

4. *How can I bring more organization to the chaos in my life?* The 7 of Cups is all about choices. The figure in the card has seven golden chalices that each represent a different desire. It's time to pick one. Make up your mind.

5. *What beauty is already around me that I'm missing?* The Ace of Pentacles is all about bringing ideas, hopes,

and dreams into fruition in the material world. We can make beautiful things. We can create beauty and joy in our lives if we push past our fears and let go of everything that's trying to get in the way.

MAY DARK MOON

Keywords
Overindulgence, excess, poison, myopia

Questions to Ponder
Consider the following as you shuffle your deck. As we observe the dance we do to avoid or engage with our shadow, it's useful to stop and ask ourselves why. What are we doing? For whom? For what purpose? Why are we doing the things we're doing? Maybe we haven't thought about these things for a long time and it's become a habit without a cause. Or maybe we're faking it until we make it

with something that never quite jelled with us, but we're afraid to let it go. This is a good time to take a fearless look at the why of our processes as well as the processes themselves.

Where are our weak spots regarding how we interact with others? What fear is driving any "bad boss" behavior? What demon is hiding in the bushes that we need to flush out and get a look at? What's driving the need to avoid self-examination? What's fueling the Harum-Scarum Overdo-Mobile? When we slow down and actually look at what's driving us to engage in reckless behavior, what do we find? How can we take advantage of the natural energies of the dark moons to evaluate and reset our behaviors?

Spread
After shuffling, draw four cards and lay them out according to the following diagram.

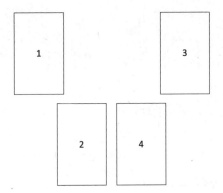

Positions

1. *Where do I overdo it, whether I see it or not?* Where are my blind spots? When it comes to this kind of thing, it can be really helpful to have someone else, or in this case the Tarot, help us take a look in the mirror. The Tarot is rather like a mirror anyway, so using it as such makes sense. With this card we're not attempting to discern why we have a certain blind spot, and we're certainly not passing any kind of judgment on ourselves or anyone else for having it; we're just trying to identify what we can't see any other way.

2. *Why is that?* What truth am I avoiding in this way? This is the card that will help us look at why we're not able to see our shadow, and what we're hiding from in a larger sense. What is the bigger truth we haven't been able to face? What are we running from?

3. *What "volume" do I need to reduce so that I can hear my heart speak?* Have you ever been told to listen for that still, small voice? I admit I have difficulty with that instruction myself, to be honest. What does that voice sound like? Where is it—or rather, where can I hear it best? Have you ever seen those old movies with people huddled around a radio and someone is turning a dial very slowly so that the voice coming over the airwaves can be heard clearly amidst the static? This is what this card is getting at: How can you tune the dial of your heart's voice to move past the static of daily life and clarify the powerful but quiet message you need to hear?

4. *What help do I have?* This is one of my favorite questions to ask the Tarot. It's useful to know what allies are available to help you face whatever shadow you need to face. Is it a spirit assist you need? Or perhaps something more earthbound, like a search engine? Or maybe even a

library, a teacher, or a trusted friend? Where can you go for help on this?

Sample Reading

In looking at the spread as a whole, we see that each card in the bottom row is a single figure, and the cards in the upper row are double figures. Three of the cards are court cards (two Knights and a King), and the fourth card is a Major Arcana card. All the suits and both arcana are represented except Pentacles, although the Pentacles are represented in the Magician card, so there's at least a little Earth energy present here. Using this deck gives us a multi-gender reading. I tend to read the energies of the Knights by their occupation as "seekers" rather than by their gender representation, but in this spread it might be useful to note the amount of "go, go, go" action energy that aligns with a more traditional definition of the masculine gender. It can also be informative to note whether the figures in the cards are looking at or away from one another, or whether they are gazing outward at something that we cannot see. These details can show us a balanced viewpoint and energy flowing together from various sources, or perhaps the energies blocking and crossing one another, thereby making connection and comprehension difficult.

1. ***Where do I overdo it, whether I see it or not?*** The Knight of Cups carries the heart's blood, the heart's truest desire in the great chalice of the Cups. If we are the Knight here, we have to ask ourselves how our constant, careful focus is harming us in some way. This is a time to get grounded again, to put the chalice down and call on the power of the Magician to help us regroup and find a way back into the physical world.

2. ***Why is that?*** The Magician tells us we are responsible for our lives. We're responsible for what we do, how we react, what dance we make and unmake. Stay focused on what's

real, what's here, what's absolutely in the now, no matter how much it frightens us. As above, so below.

3. *What "volume" do I need to reduce so that I can hear my heart speak?* The Knight of Wands talks about excitement and adventure and the wild ride promised by escape. The work that we need to be doing is not glamorous, though. It's sweaty, dedicated, and relentless, so let's get down to it and leave the wild drama for another day.

4. *What help do I have?* The King of Swords is clarity and farsightedness personified in the Tarot. He perceives problems before they arise and can think up solutions in the blink of an eye. Having him on your side to help you think in new, creative ways is a blessing and a gift.

KNIGHT OF CUPS

Knight of Wands

THE MAGICIAN

KING OF SWORDS

June

THE FULL MOON

Western culture has a rich and varied relationship with the month of June. Because the weather is traditionally lovely in so many places, June is ideal for celebrating outdoor weddings, hand-fastings, proposals, betrothals, and even the beginning of barbecue and picnic season. Flowers are in bloom, trees are in full leaf and provide ample shade, the bright colors shimmer in the sunlight, and the temperature is not yet so hot as to be uncomfortable. It's also the end of many a traditional school year and the harbinger of a summer of free exploration, adventure, relaxation, and release. Many schools graduate their seniors in June, adding to the sense of freedom, expansion, and possibility. There are also many other reasons to celebrate in June: Juneteenth is a national holiday in the United States commemorating June 19, 1865, when the last group of the nation's African slaves were notified of their freedom under the Emancipation Proclamation; and in remembrance of the Stonewall riots that began on June 28, 1969, the entire month of June marks a worldwide celebration of LGBTQ+ pride, culminating in parades and parties on the last weekend of the month.

June can also be a sort of "treasure month," bringing up special properties and influences that can help you through a rough patch when you weren't really anticipating it. A benefit of our increasingly global agricultural economy is being able to buy strawberries from markets and fruit stands during many months of the year, but this wasn't always a possibility. Strawberries used to be harvested in June (hence the month's full-moon nickname, the Strawberry Moon) and were only available for a very short time afterwards. If you got the chance to enjoy fresh strawberries, especially with a dish of cream and maybe a little sugar, you were very lucky, indeed.

Amidst all this activity, it's important to remember that going full speed trying to do everything may mean that you're not fully present for all of it. Fatigue, depression, overwhelm—these are all real things, as is FOMO ("fear of missing out" for my folks who don't do acronyms). Nobody likes to be left out, but being discerning in how and when we celebrate and knowing what invitations to say "no, thank you" to is part of growing up. June can be a good time to begin thinking about how and when to prune those events and activities—and perhaps even people—who do not add to your joyful celebration of life. That's not carte blanche to be rude or condescending, but rather a call to remember that reciprocity is a key element of participating in society. We give joy, and we receive joy from others who are celebrating. We suffer, and we receive empathetic understanding of our suffering from others who know what it feels like. We don't do anyone any favors if we're just taking up space, rather than being fully awake and ourselves as we share and celebrate their experiences of life, and they ours.

The Full Moon—Southern Hemisphere

As the celebrations of midwinter approach and the calls of friends and family tend toward more indoor gatherings and activities (unless you have access to snow or ice sports and you enjoy participating in them), how can you protect yourself against overdoing it and focus instead on the richest, most heart-centered experiences, rather than on keeping up with the Joneses?

THE DARK MOON

June is a time of warming days, schedules changing, kids going to camp, lovers getting married. In the Northern Hemisphere, June means the beginning of summer. Summer can mean vacations, breaks from routine, leaving work and difficulty behind and breezing off to someplace fun, moving from an established pattern of imposing order on chaos into a more relaxed and friendlier "live and let live" attitude. And even if there's no vacation or break—even when all summer means is sleeveless shirts or khaki pants or remembering to put on sunblock and a hat before leaving the house—as the days get longer and begin to get hot and bright, summer still marks a difference in attitude, a potential willingness to play and celebrate with others (or on our own, if that's our preference). But as with every other month or season, there's a shadow side to June. This playfulness can tend toward anarchy, and the need for a break or a change can turn the mildest person into a tyrant. Social pressure and the increasingly ubiquitous FOMO we get from social media can drive us to make it look like we're having fun on that much-needed vacation when in fact all we're doing is changing our backdrop, and we're not really disconnecting at all.

The Dark Moon—Southern Hemisphere

In the dark of winter, the natural world is quiet, and we may not have community around us to mirror our experiences back to us. Perhaps our circumstances are such that we're alone during the darkest nights of the year. At this time of the year, we have a rich opportunity to ask ourselves who we are in the darkness, without interference or distraction from outside. If we do have family and friends around us, it might still be easier to see our true selves under June's dark moon, because it gives us an excuse to move away from noise or disruption toward silence and peace so that we can touch the dark moon's energy and learn from it.

JUNE FULL MOON

Keywords

Commitment, freedom, order, decisions

Questions to Ponder

Consider the following as you shuffle your deck. What does this full moon reveal about what can be released, either because it's not going to succeed or because it's directing energy and influence away from something more important? What promises are we making now? What is beginning and what is ending? What partnerships have we begun and which ones have we ended, whether we meant to or not? What do we need to focus on now as the growing season begins in earnest?

Spread

After shuffling, draw six cards and lay them out according to the following diagram.

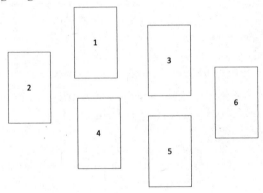

Positions

1. *What is blossoming most fully for me now and needs my complete attention?* It's so easy at this time of the year to become distracted by all sorts of responsibilities and needs, some belonging to others to whom we're responsible and some belonging to us. But this full Strawberry Moon is calling on us to focus. It would be wonderful if we could do and be all things all the time everywhere to all people, but we can't. To be human is to have choice, which means you have to decide.

2. *What can be pruned back, either to be developed at a later time or to be composted and built upon in the future?* This is the flipside of the previous question, and we should consider it carefully because it's important not to throw the baby out with the bathwater. But what needs to be let go of? What can be released, if not permanently, then at least for now? Something has been taking up too much focus and too much space, and it needs to shuffle on out the door.

3. *What connections and harmonious energies are available for me to begin working with now?* Once we've done the heavy lifting of actually choosing what to focus on and what to release, it can be refreshing and helpful to reach out either for help in next steps or just to share what we've done. This particular card will indicate where to look for community—or, perhaps more importantly, where *not* to look.

4. *What have I learned so far that I can manifest and share with my community?* Finding and sharing with our people can be a wonderful, even transformative experience. But sometimes it can be a challenge to know what we have to share. Finding focus for ourselves is one thing, but sharing our intention, our work, and our wisdom with others is something else. It takes bravery and determination and confidence in ourselves and our chosen work. How can we best manifest this and make it useful both for ourselves and for others?

5. *Where do I need to overcome restriction and let myself celebrate and enjoy the goodness around me?* For many people this can be a big challenge. Honestly, it was easier for me to shove, lift, mangle, wrangle, and wrestle my monstrously heavy futon bed up a flight of stairs and into my apartment than it was for me to sleep in it that night

after my ludicrous exertions. I mean, why in the world didn't I ask for help? This is my dilemma. Let the energy of this full moon show you where you can relax a little and not do everything yourself. Where can you celebrate a bit more, and how? And remember, celebration is different for everyone. If a big party stresses you out, don't go to it. Don't throw one. Let the cards show you what real celebration means to you.

6. *What full-moon magic is here for me now that brings the energy of simple, natural, luxurious abundance that I might have overlooked before?* It doesn't have to be whatever society tells us "luxury" is. Like celebration, true luxury is different for everyone, and we can take this time to find out what it is and how to enjoy it for ourselves. Letting go of how other people define states of being is a luxury, indeed.

Sample Reading

There are contrasts and consistencies throughout this spread. The stability of the King of Pentacles contrasts with the chaos of the 5 of Wands; the 8 of Cups and the 3 of Wands hold the same position physically, although the former is moving forward and the latter holding still. The masked figure in the 5 of Cups contrasts with the clear-eyed regard of the King of Pentacles, and the wild speed of the Knight of Swords practically flies around all the other cards whether they're moving or not. So it would be valuable for us, as we review the spread, to see what's clearly visible, and also to think about how each question connects to the others, to see whether there are contrasting elements or consistencies to strengthen the wisdom we receive.

1. *What is blossoming most fully for me now and needs my complete attention?* The 5 of Cups is often seen as a card of mourning, but I think a more important and pertinent

interpretation of it is as a card of focus. The 5 of Cups in this position tells us that what is blossoming most fully in life is literally and metaphorically what we're *not* looking at. We are being called to turn away from the way things used to be because there's literally nothing there for us. The future and all its possibilities lie ahead.

2. *What can be pruned back, either to be developed at a later time or to be composted and built upon in the future?* The King of Pentacles is the master of the Earth element, so it is his purview to know everything about the material world and how it operates. Draw boundaries and hold them, because if you don't, you'll get flooded with emotions and practices of the past that might not even be yours.

3. *What connections and harmonious energies are available for me to begin working with now?* The 8 of Cups is the wisdom in the third position, showing us what harmonious energies are available for us to start working with now. The emphasis here is also on leaving, on moving into a new realm of emotional resonance and understanding. It's time to leave what you know and search for greener pastures elsewhere. Those harmonious energies are out there somewhere, waiting. Go find them!

4. *What have I learned so far that I can manifest and share with my community?* The Knight of Swords moves at the speed of thought and is a brilliant advocate for his ideas. As you travel along this new path, share your thoughts and ideas with others. Let your honest, authentic voice be heard.

5. *Where do I need to overcome restriction and let myself celebrate and enjoy the goodness around me?* The 3 of Wands shows us where and how to move past restrictions.

It's important at this stage to not flinch when things start to work out, and to not engage in self-sabotage. See what's coming for what it really is, and accept it as it comes.

6. *What full-moon magic is here for me now that brings the energy of simple, natural, luxurious abundance that I might have overlooked before?* The 5 of Wands reminds us that not all gatherings are going to be fun or easy, but sometimes challenging conversations or arguments are exactly what's needed to clear the air. Sometimes we need other people's perspectives and energy to create what we can't create on our own.

JUNE DARK MOON

Keywords

Tyranny, chaos, confusion, negativity

Questions to Ponder

Consider the following as you shuffle your deck. Are we being real with ourselves, or are we putting on a show? Do we warm others with our summer light or blind them with it? As we celebrate the events of June, or as others celebrate around us, do we share joy or do we let ourselves become tyrants in our expectations?

Spread

After shuffling, draw five cards and lay them out according to the following diagram.

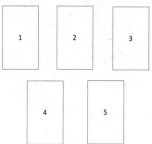

Positions

1. *What kind of "break-taker" am I, really?* When it comes time to go on a holiday or take a break, do we work at it as if we're at work and never really rest at all? Do we work hard at relaxing because we don't really know how to let go? Or are we the opposite, the kind of break-taker who blows off all responsibility completely in favor of escaping into the moment?

2. *What turns my joy to sorrow?* Do I "should" myself to death? Do I get myself worked up because whatever plans I have aren't as fabulous as someone else's? Do I

bring my unresolved suffering with me wherever I go like an uninvited guest?

3. ***How can I turn it back?*** What actions can I take to release some of this suffering, to honor the shadow of the moment, and let it go so that joy can find its way in?

4. ***How can I shift any negative tendencies I have when it comes to celebrating other people's joy?*** Where can I work on being compassionate toward myself and everyone else and just be present in the moment? What can I release that is keeping me from feeling and sharing the joy of the community around me?

5. ***What is the dark moon's message for me now?*** What is it saying that I need to know, so that I can move forward with confidence and strong belief in myself?

Sample Reading

There's a nice flow here from darkness into light, from a fraught period of trauma into a smoother time of connection and heart-centered enjoyment. As we move through the reading, a blast of full sunshine from the Sun redirects us from being stuck in our heads (the 6 and 10 of Swords) into the heart space (the Page and 2 of Cups).

1. ***What kind of "break-taker" am I, really?*** The 6 of Swords tells us we aren't the happiest travelers in town, not by a long shot. We travel light and may tend to be a little grim in our approach to relaxation. Our thoughts and worries, perhaps our past experiences, all get in the way of having a good time.

2. ***What turns my joy to sorrow?*** The 10 of Swords. We can't perceive joy at all because of the anxieties and thoughts going through our heads a mile a minute. What

joy we have is drained away by our inability to see that we are not our thoughts.

3. ***How can I turn it back?*** The Sun helps us throw some light on the situation! What makes us happy? What brings the sun into our lives in a good way? Life is a dangerous business whether we're enjoying ourselves or not, so why not enjoy ourselves while we can? Lighten up!

4. ***How can I shift any negative tendencies I have when it comes to celebrating other people's joy?*** The Page of Cups. Talk to each other from a heart-centered place and let go of any preconceived notions about how people are feeling. Release the expectation that we somehow know what others are going through, and let them tell us their stories for themselves.

5. ***What is the dark moon's message for me now?*** The 2 of Cups brings a message from the June dark moon. Connection is not only possible, it's meant to be. Once we learn to start talking to each other and really listening to each other's truth, we will begin to make connections that matter and that will last.

Summer Solstice

Keywords
Balance, tipping point, flow, light

*H*ave you ever noticed how nothing in life is a straight line? Everything seems to rise and fall, expand and contract, move forward, move back, but never ever stay still or move directly from Point A to Point B—unless we have a pencil and ruler and draw a line to those exact coordinates. And even if we do, nothing happens once the line is drawn. It just sits there, unmoving, without flow or energy, lifeless until we add a curve or an angle or some other shift that provides movement and, somehow, change. It's one of life's great mysteries, the how and why of things changing, and how to live with the dreadful consequences of not allowing a thing to change because we hope to keep it as we find it. But that's not what life is—everything changes constantly, all the time. Well, almost all the time.

When we approach the solstices of the year, we come to a point of stillness, of perfect balance between these roiling shifts between times, a moment when we can pause in silence and contemplate before the next step or leap or dance into the future. In the Northern Hemisphere, there is more light on this day than any other day of the year. The earth has turned this side of her face to the sun, and after the passage of the Summer Solstice in the north, the light will begin to fade little by little, moving past the point of balance back into darkness as the earth's southern face turns toward the sun and the light. In some places this tilt and dip brings rains and flooding, in others fires and windstorms. Where I live in the US just south of San Francisco, the Summer Solstice is often a foggy, wind-driven affair, with occasional bright sun peering through the mists and temperatures rising only as you drive farther inland away from the Pacific. The afternoon winds bring fog and moisture to earth's giant children, the redwood trees, and their fluffy open bark; but we humans had better bring extra layers no matter where we go along the coast, or risk learning firsthand the accuracy of the pithy bon mot "the coldest winter I ever spent was a summer in San Francisco."

No matter your microclimate, in the north the Summer Solstice signals a shift in the balance between light and dark. At this time, we're called on to honor the Horned God, who enriches the lives of his people until he sacrifices himself for their benefit, or the Great Goddess, who nurtures and provides for her children with breathtaking bounty, or both together when we sing the sun up on Midsummer morning to keep the Wheel turning and the energy flowing between gods and earth and people, living and dead.

Questions to Ponder

Consider the following as you shuffle your deck. As we approach the Summer Solstice and the time of pause and stillness, it's valuable to consider how we handle balance. Are we ready for our spotlight at Cirque du Soleil, or do we have a gravitational attraction to the pavement? How do we move through the world, and how does that affect our self-image and what we think we're capable of? In this moment of shifting energies, are we clear enough about what we want and need to take full advantage of it, or do we move through space numb and blind and exhausted by life? It's important to not hold judgment about this in any way, but to try to see things as they exist, unfiltered by attitudes, opinions, and beliefs. What can we leave behind as we move through this between-time? And how can we mark this passage? How do we hold ourselves in balance? Do we embrace the pause, or do we move right through it into the next moment of contrasting energy? Or are we frozen in the pause, unable to move for fear of falling, of error, of catastrophic mistake? How do we manifest the deities in our own lives, becoming our own heroes or villains?

How do we recreate the ancient stories of life and death within our own lives to help us understand how to live and thrive and succeed in an ever-changing world?

Southern Hemisphere

If it's useful for you, please feel free to switch the spreads and read the Summer Solstice one in December and the Winter Solstice one in June.

Wherever in the world we are during the June solstice, whether it's the summer or winter, the rainy season or the dry, there is an opportunity when the sun reaches its stillness point to stop along with it, to let ourselves become silent and to quiet as much as we can in our lives, to pause and wait until the moment passes. The opportunity is present to take note of what we see during this liminal time, what comes up, and what changes we notice, if any, once we start moving again.

Spread

After shuffling, draw seven cards and lay them out according to the following diagram.

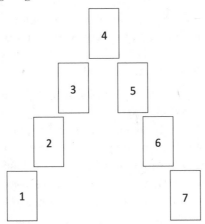

Positions

1. *What is the balance or tipping point of my life right now?* If I can identify the edge I'm walking on, it might be easier to balance myself. Maybe there are skills I have that I can use, or skills that I can develop to help myself move forward?

2. *How do I hold myself in balance?* This will be different for everybody. If you are familiar with Western astrology, you might have heard that the water-sign people do very well existing between extremes, or at least they do well around drama, and maybe some of us do. But not always,

   and not all of us. Looking at how you relate to balance can be very valuable. Is it your natural state, or do you move between a dizzying array of states of being? Do you move carefully or recklessly?

3. *What would help me get better at pausing, at taking a breath?* How do you hold space for yourself? How do you wait, take time, let yourself pause before choosing? If making choices is something you struggle with, it can help to give yourself the gift of time so that you can relax for a moment, take a breath, and release whatever tension you hold around the subject. Is there an ally in your life somewhere that can help you with this?

4. *What can I do to help turn the Wheel from light to darkness in my own life?* There are mighty forces at work in life, and humans are small in the face of them, especially during big transitions. To help support a feeling of agency, we can ask what can be done to make the great changes we want to see in our lives. At this solstice moment, what can you do as an individual in your own space to help turn the Wheel toward the sheltering time as the light fades?

5. *What can I leave behind as I move through this passage?* What do I need to let go of, either known or unknown? Perhaps you can ask what you need help with releasing instead, or what you need to release that you're not seeing. Either way, the solstice is an excellent time for focusing on letting go of the past.

6. *How can I take advantage of this in-between space?* Liminal spaces can be very useful for changing our positions, opinions, or ideas or taking in new information. We can meet new people, experience ourselves in new ways, and change our minds about how we see things. So ask yourself how you can best take advantage of this in-between space as you move forward on your journey.

7. *What message can I take away from this Summer Solstice?* What do I most need to know as I take a step forward into the next unknown? No matter what else is going on or what has happened before, a new page is turning now. What will help us take the best possible advantage of it?

Sample Reading

Perhaps one of the most interesting things about this draw is the lack of Major Arcana cards, considering how powerful and significant a tipping point the solstices are. And yet we have cards that reflect the everyday activities, stresses, worries, and successes we all can relate to because we've all been there. It's a profoundly human thing, being on a balance point between the past and the future and not knowing whether to step forward carefully or to leap with complete abandon. Who knows what the results of that step will be? Here in this draw we see family, connection, home, sovereignty, and choices—all the things that make up a move between what was and what will be. We also see that all the numbers in this spread are even: 10, 4, 6, and 8. Consider what those numbers mean to you. In my practice, if I'm asking a yes/no question with a roll of the dice, I assign a "no" meaning to odd numbers and a "yes" meaning to even numbers. This can add an extra layer to your divination, especially if there's a yes/no question underlying it. In this case, when we look at this spread for the Summer Solstice, we can think of it in terms of a cosmic "yes" in favor of forward movement once we step beyond the tipping point into action.

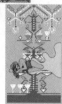

1. *What is the balance or tipping point of my life right now?* The 10 of Cups. The issues and questions surrounding the needs of family (of choice or of birth) and the needs of the self are prominent right now. Balance is required so that we do what's needful for others without sacrificing our own needs.

2. *How do I hold myself in balance?* The King of Pentacles illuminates how we hold ourselves in this balancing act between personal and familial obligations. The King of Pentacles is kind yet firm, a ruler who shows us how to hold boundaries without becoming sharp, angry, or threatening when we must say "no."

3. *What would help me get better at pausing, at taking a breath?* The 4 of Wands shows us how to act decisively to shelter and protect our boundaries and to make sure that we feel safe enough to make important decisions wisely—without acting from impulse or a frantic sense of necessity. Boundaries are the key here.

4. *What can I do to help turn the Wheel from light to darkness in my own life?* The 6 of Pentacles is a card of giving and receiving. When we ask how we can help turn the Wheel, we are told to give and to receive. Help others where you can, but remember that allowing others to help you is also a gift to them.

5. *What can I leave behind as I move through this passage?* The 4 of Cups reveals what we need to let go of as we move into the future. Cynicism is a trap, and this card is full of it: cynicism, lethargy, seeing the world through sarcasm-colored glasses. Change is inevitable though, whether we want it or not—do we acknowledge the change and embrace it, or keep waiting for something better?

6. *How can I take advantage of this in-between space?* The 8 of Cups. It's time to explore new ways of expressing ourselves and new realms of emotion and connection. New horizons await, and now is the perfect time to move toward them. Let the power of the turning Wheel propel you forward.

7. *What message can I take away from this Summer Solstice?* The Page of Pentacles. The pages in the Tarot are all messengers, so we're being asked to pay attention here. Don't be afraid to do the work; there's nothing to be afraid of there, not really. Perfection is a non-entity; it's something some of us use to scare ourselves into inaction, but it's ok to make mistakes, to fall over, to break, and to mend.

July

THE FULL MOON

There's a ferocity about the month of July that brings up all kinds of ideas. In the United States we celebrate our independence in July, and the French also have been known to raise a glass to the revolution on Quatorze Juillet. It's high summer in the Northern Hemisphere, and the power of the sun is on full display. But it's not all picnics and flag-waving, either. Revolutions and uprisings are messy and loud, and people get hurt. Fireworks look pretty from a distance, but get too close and they're just so much mortar fire when really all a person wants is a hot dog, an ear of corn, and a quiet place to look at the stars. Pet stores do a brisk business selling special garments to help pets feel safe during fireworks season, and anyone who suffers from any kind of anxiety or PTSD also might not enjoy the week or two of nightly "earth-shattering kabooms."

But if we think about what these occasions are meant to commemorate, and what position they hold within the Wheel of the Year, we can get beyond the considerations of borders and boundaries and think about what the Buck Moon heralds in our own lives. In addition to the man-made noise of July, there are also thunderstorms that bring lightning, lashing rain, and winds. Then quiet and peace. Expansion and contraction. Noise, then silence. As we go through this stage of reaching out for new ways of being, then pulling back to regroup, then reaching out again, we can ask ourselves: What does our own independence look like? Where do we draw our boundaries, and how do we defend them? Do we fight for our right to exist, or do we let ourselves get run over by the crowd?

The male deer is an independent creature, moving through the forest quietly but with direction and purpose. He watches and knows what goes on around him and can smell trouble a mile off. Deer in general are gentle and non-aggressive, but the males will fight over access to females—the "rut," it's called. You can hear the crashing antlers of battling males miles off. It may seem silly or overwrought to go to such lengths instead of moving on to find more accessible or less powerfully defended females, but the males are fighting for the right to survive, to procreate, to be. Maybe it's the same when people fight for independence, whether literally or metaphorically, collectively or individually. We fight for the right to be, to stand up as ourselves and be counted and to have our values validated, respected, and passed down to our descendants with honor.

The Full Moon—Southern Hemisphere

Consider what your independence looks like. It might not be a good time of year to be firing up the barbecue and having a block party, but you can still consider how you celebrate freedom—or do you celebrate it at all? Is it perhaps something that you take for granted? How do you define your freedom, and does considering your boundaries and those of other people change that definition?

THE DARK MOON

When we work with July's dark moon, the shadow energy around issues of independence and individuality comes up loud and large. Our tendencies to be our own selves can turn us dictatorial if we're not careful, mindful of our intent, and willing to look hard at our responsibility for where we are and what our lives look like. Have we set up boundaries that are so strong they're more like prison walls than healthy borders? Do we repel others willfully and run roughshod over someone else's boundaries simply because they disagree with us? Or do we withdraw entirely into our own space and reject the outside world and all its activities, good and bad, because we're frightened or overwhelmed, or because we just don't want to do the work involved in connecting with others in a healthy way?

Whereas the full moons of the upcoming harvest months give us the opportunity to celebrate community and our individual place within it, the contraction of the July dark moon is an opportunity to see where we take our authority for granted, where we assume that our voices are the most important in the room or that we are the only ones who can deliver the message that needs sending. For example, as a white woman living in the United States, I can reflect on how people who look like me allow ourselves to become weaponized in body and mind against those who are struggling for justice. More broadly, this dark moon is a perfect time for those of us who were born into the oppressor class to look hard at how we center our own voices in a crowd and expect to be heard, and how we can instead take advantage of the opportunity to use that power to hold space for historically oppressed groups to come forward and be heard. If this specific instance of self-contraction for the greater good doesn't apply to you, this dark moon energy is still great for working with shadow energies around your relationship to power, authority, and authenticity.

The Dark Moon—Southern Hemisphere

The questions about power and authority absolutely translate and are useful to consider as the year is in its dark cycle. Consider how you conserve resources: where you are being careful versus where you might be behaving selfishly from a place of fear.

JULY FULL MOON

Keywords

Storms, revolution, strength, independence

Questions to Ponder

Consider the following as you shuffle your deck. Think about what independence means. Think about what nation and country means, and where we find ourselves fitting into it. How are we free, and how are we not? Did you know that Frederick Douglass gave a speech in July 1852 entitled "What to the Slave is the Fourth of July?" challenging the celebration of the United States as the land of the free while slavery still existed? Have we considered what our blind spots might be when it comes to the meaning of independence and freedom for all?

Spread

After shuffling, draw five cards and lay them out according to the following diagram.

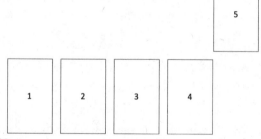

Positions

1. *How can I declare my independence?* We all know what we would do if only everything was perfect and the timing was right. We would stand up in some grand, dramatic way and make our declaration, and we'd get cheers and applause and maybe even a movie made about our bravery. But it's not like that in real life. Standing up for ourselves can be challenging and uncomfortable, and maybe even painful if we have a history of trauma or abuse. So how can we make our declaration or develop our constitution of the self safely but proudly, and with

strength and commitment? What can help us focus our intention so that we don't get distracted?

2. ***What are the biggest storms that hold me back?*** Speaking of distractions, where are the storms coming from? Are they the kind of storms that you can feel building over time, or are they the storms that sort of explode out of nowhere, rain or hail like hell for twenty minutes, and then vanish? Are they emotional storms, or are they the kind of storms that our minds kick up when we're confused? Is it a physical manifestation of confusion and strife? Finding a way to identify where the problem areas are can help us prepare for storms before they hit. We can't ever stop them—storm gotta storm, after all—but we can get ourselves ready to weather them better, and maybe even get to a point where we might try dancing in the rain a little!

3. ***What new boundaries need to be declared and held?*** Once we make our declaration of self-determination, where do we need to shore up our defenses? How can we best protect the new precious thing we've created? Because we need to protect it—nobody else is going to, and there are those who might try to breach our new defenses.

4. ***What old boundaries need to be overcome?*** In order to establish new boundaries, we might have to destroy some old ones. We may need to clear some ground to make space for our new self-determination. So what needs to go? Do we need to wipe out old ways of thinking? Or do we need to change how we do things or how we present ourselves in the world? What blocks our development into whatever new way we're trying to create? Is there a dead tree blocking our new sapling from the sun? What is the obstacle and how can we remove it safely?

5. *What does my personal Flag of Freedom look like?* Sometimes we need to just stand up and announce that things are not going to be as they were. Sometimes just making changes quietly won't do; we need to make a splash, and it's absolutely ok to do so! But if we're not used to splash-making, how can we do it in a way that's most authentic to ourselves and our new intention? What is the new face we want to show the world? What are our new symbols, words, and colors?

Sample Reading

It's lovely when all the suits are represented in a spread. There's something balanced about it, as the combined presence of Pentacles (Earth), Swords (Air), Wands (Fire), and Cups (Water) breathes Spirit into the whole. Maybe it's a witchy thing: I have Norse runes representing each of the elements tattooed on four of my fingers, two on each hand, and when I put my hands together it's like a circuit is completing itself. It's the same with this spread: Earth (the 9 and 3 of Pentacles) and Air (the King of Swords) are on either side of Water (the Ace of Cups), and Fire (the 9 of Wands) reigns above. They all pull together to complete the circuit of the heart, pressing us on toward freedom.

1. *How can I declare my independence?* The 9 of Pentacles is a card of discernment, of peaceful knowing, and trusting in one's choices. Maybe this declaration of independence needs to be something personal, something directed at the self? Our freedom is not something that is yet to be, it's something that already is.

2. *What are the biggest storms that hold me back?* The 3 of Pentacles shows that in doing the work of developing the self, having too much input from outside sources is not a good thing. This card reinforces the idea that independence is just that: freedom of the self

from overwhelming community influences so that the individual can develop in peace.

3. ***What new boundaries need to be declared and held?*** The Ace of Cups says that learning to say "no" with loving firmness and conviction is a skill that must be developed in order to protect the growing self. The heart is the most precious thing, and it deserves our full and undivided attention.

4. ***What old boundaries need to be overcome?*** The King of Swords indicates here that we need to change our minds. New governing principles are needed. Break down your old governing principles in favor of a new way of sheltering and creating boundaries around the precious thing that is revealed in the third card, and don't let your Brain-King talk you out of it.

5. ***What does my personal Flag of Freedom look like?*** The 9 of Wands shows us a figure who is proud and defiant, maybe a bit wounded but stronger for it. Burdens have been turned into strengths, and wisdom has been used to set up a boundary fence to keep destructive forces out of the new land beyond. Our flag tells others we will always fight for who we are.

ACE OF CUPS   KING OF SWORDS

JULY DARK MOON

Keywords
Authority issues, boundaries, resources

Questions to Ponder
Consider the following as you shuffle your deck. What is our relationship to power, and how do we reflect that within ourselves, in our relationships, and in how we connect with our Higher Power? Do we transfer responsibility for our actions and choices onto an authority that is beyond our control? Are we hiding behind our boundaries?

Spread
After shuffling, draw four cards and lay them out according to the following diagram.

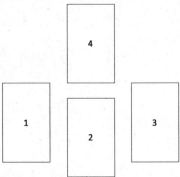

Positions
1. *What is my relationship to power?* Under what circumstances do I become a tyrant, or, conversely, when do I let myself become a victim? Sometimes when we work with others our old conditioning comes out, and we approach getting what we want as if it needs to be a fight. We get ourselves all worked up, and what could have been a win-win if we'd worked with others as peers and equals

instead becomes a situation where someone has to lose and someone has to win. Maybe we can learn to use our power to release ourselves from the need to be in charge in that way. Can we let go of that conditioning and see power as a tool and not a weapon?

2. ***Where do I take my authority for granted?*** Do I present myself in community as if I am the most important person in the room? How do I see myself in relationship to other people when it comes to deciding who gets to be heard? If we are used to being listened to, it might be very difficult to not take it personally when asked to step back and let someone else be centered. Can we take that opportunity to learn and listen?

3. ***How have I imprisoned myself?*** Have I created boundaries built on ideas about self-worth and self-esteem that are so strong and deeply ingrained that I cannot get past them in order to hear and respect others, especially if we disagree? What do my boundaries really look like?

4. ***How can I use my power and strength for the good of all?*** How can I let go of whatever victim mentality I might have, and use my privilege to help others?

Sample Reading

I was lucky enough to be in a class taught by Rachel Pollack at the Northwest Tarot Symposium (NWTS) right before the pandemic started, and she spoke about the 10 of Pentacles in a way I'll never forget. She described it as showing a scene from *The Odyssey*, one of Western culture's oldest stories, when Odysseus comes home from the wars and no one but the dog recognizes him because he's been gone for so long. The energy of the 10 of Pentacles is very much like that, even without a dog in the card: home and family are connections we can't shake. We're rooted to our people for better or worse, and the 10 of Pentacles roots the spread in the same way.

1. *What is my relationship to power?* The 7 of Wands defends herself from a position of strength. The shadow side of this kind of relationship to power and authority, however, is that there's not a lot of nuance going on—a certain self-reliance might border on loneliness and maybe an unwillingness to trust others to get the work done.

2. *Where do I take my authority for granted?* The 10 of Pentacles represents a complex web of community relationships. What we think we are now can change in an instant, or it can be worn away into nothing by time. Take nothing for granted, especially the people in your life. And your fur babies—don't forget your fur babies.

3. *How have I imprisoned myself?* The 6 of Cups. If we are locked behind a door, it's possible that it can only be opened by going back to go forward, that continuing to try to force it open is frustrating and dangerous. Consider perhaps that the past may provide the key we need to unlock the door in front of us. Sometimes approaching current problems with the playful hearts we had as children is all it takes to find a way to unlock that door and move on.

4. *How can I use my power and strength for the good of all?* The 4 of Pentacles tells us that maybe we've been too quick to give it all away. It's telling us to be solid and well-grounded in our lives and our environments so that we're able to stay strong and healthy, which in turn will put us in a better position to help others in the long run.

Lammas / Lúnasa

Keywords

Early harvest, nutrition, future glimpses, doing the work

Lammas (or "loaf mass" in medieval English) is the first of the three harvest festivals of the witch's year. It's a celebration of the first grains with which bread is baked and presented to the community and the gods, in a church at mass or around a ritual bonfire or hearth, depending on when and where you are and what faith you practice. While we may not be quite as agrarian a society these days as we used to be, Lammas is still celebrated as a time of joy and prayers for a good harvest—of whatever kind—to last the community throughout the coming winter. Abundance of summer fruits, fish, meats, the first grains, and the blessings of community and connection are all celebrated with feasting and dancing, rituals and parties. We honor bread, the staff of life, the work of our hands that keeps famine from our door. We offer bread, which in many various ways and traditions is broken to ensure togetherness and peaceful community. We create bread, a staple of the Western diet, which can be the easiest thing in the world to make and the hardest to make properly. On Lammas we celebrate being alive and together, and we recognize that the cold days are coming, and that after celebration comes preparation.

Lammas is also the first of the great fire festivals of the witch's year. In this context it can be referred to by its Irish name, Lúnasa, the "month of August," on the first day of which is the festival of the great Irish sun god Lugh. On August 1, wherever you live in the Northern Hemisphere, it's probably going to be hot and getting hotter through the dog days of summer. The fire of Lúnasa isn't just implied in the weather, though. It's a reminder that darkness is coming, and that creating community in times of light is important so that it will be there for us in the dark. We must do the work—sow, plant, till the soil, and harvest the grain—in order to have food to last us through lean times. Doing the work together makes it easier for everyone, and it means that everyone has a chance to survive.

Questions to Ponder

Consider the following as you shuffle your deck. How's it going with this year's "harvest"? The ideas, plans, and projects that we had at the beginning of the year, those seeds we planted—how are they doing now? Think back: Where did we want to be by now, and where are we according to that metric? What are we not seeing that we should be? Which goals or projects need some extra attention? What needs to be pruned so that stronger roots can grow and mature? What has turned out the way we thought it would, and what has absolutely not gone according to plan? And is that ok? Sometimes the plan that goes completely pear-shaped is the one that gets us across obstacles we didn't foresee. And let's not forget about the communal aspect of the harvest: Does anybody around us need a little help with their work?

Now is also the time to ask ourselves what nourishes us. What is that thing without which we would wither and fade away? For many of us, our relationship with food can be cranky and complicated, so we should allow ourselves to consider what nourishment really means to us without reference (if possible) to all those glorious carbs that can be so good at helping us numb out when things get to be too much. If we are feeding ourselves unhealthy food, is there a reason for that? And we should think about how we celebrate community with food: Do we feed our neighborhood? Are we the hosts whose parties always end up in the kitchen?

Southern Hemisphere

If it's useful for you, please feel free to switch the spreads and read the Imbolg one in August and the Lúnasa one in February.

For you, this is the time when seeds begin to be planted, when the newness of life begins to emerge from whatever your winter looks like. It may only be hints and promises, but it can give you an idea of where things might go from here. Take careful note at this time of what has survived the winter and what can be composted to help the survivors grow and thrive. What needs attention and what can be released?

Spread

After shuffling, draw five cards and lay them out according to the following diagram.

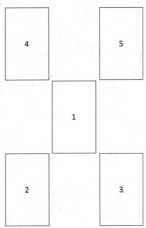

Positions

1. *What is my "staff of life," that thing without which I would falter and fade?* This is the thing that is foundational to you, that thing around which all your harvests exist. It's what you're fighting for and what's most precious to you.

2. ***Where am I right now regarding my personal harvest for the year?*** This is a check-in to see how you're doing compared with your plans from earlier in the year. It can also be a card of general reflection, a sort of temperature-check for what's going on in your life right now.

3. ***What needs to be pruned?*** What can you let go of? Or perhaps more importantly, what do you actively need to remove? Weeds won't go away because we let them go. Weeds—or any plant or thought or plan that is not useful or is perhaps actively threatening to that piece that *does* need to survive—must be actively fought against and removed. It's not enough to release the idea. Work must be done in the manifest world to clear out what isn't helping or is actively harmful.

4. ***What needs some extra attention?*** What needs the light of the sun, the fire of creation and liveliness and nourishment, to help it thrive? For some plans or ideas, simple maintenance is required. But maybe your plan or project isn't as simple as you thought, and it needs revision. Where do you need to go back to the beginning and review how well things have been working (or not working)?

5. ***How am I doing right now with community relationships and connections?*** We are social animals and we need each other to survive. Given that, and given wherever you are at the moment, how are you managing connections? Could you be doing more, or do you need to be doing less? Sometimes our own situation is so overwhelming and frightening that the only way to deal with it is by not dealing with it, by prioritizing others and ignoring our own problems. This is a temporary fix, though. We can't (or shouldn't) make a practice of prioritizing others over ourselves all the time. Where are you on this spectrum?

Sample Reading

When we look at this spread as a whole, we can see a lot of big energies represented by the three Major Arcana cards (the Tower, the Chariot, and Strength). They surround the Ace at the center, the smallest first step of any journey, the source. It's also interesting that we see a lot of Earth (Pentacles) and Fire around the watery Ace (two of the Major Arcana cards below the Ace of Cups show fire: the fire of lightning in the Tower and the fire of forward movement in the Chariot). We don't see any Swords (Air) here, but there are of course airy notes in the stars in the veil of the Chariot, as well as in the fact that both the female figure in the Strength card and the charioteer are controlling animals with their minds; note that the charioteer isn't using a whip or reins. But there are no Swords cards here, indicating that the realm of the mind is being worked too hard. This spread's focus is on the body and the heart.

1. *What is my "staff of life," that thing without which I would falter and fade?* The Ace of Cups. This card is the Blessing Cup, the flowing heart of the Tarot. If we remember that no matter what we are harvesting, we come from a place of love, and if we're honest with ourselves about how we manage the workings of love in our lives, we cannot go wrong.

2. *Where am I right now regarding my personal harvest for the year?* The Tower is a card of great disruption and upheaval. It brings change into our lives whether we want it to or not. In answer to the question of how we're doing with regard to our personal yearly "harvest," it's easy to see that it's all gone rather spectacularly to hell.

3. *What needs to be pruned?* The Chariot is the card of victory and forward movement. However, the position is asking what needs to be cut away, stopped, for the good of the whole process. Is it possible to stop going? It is,

actually, and we're being reminded to focus less on the goal and pay more attention to how we're getting there.

4. ***What needs some extra attention?*** Strength. Have we tried to be too strong for too long? Do a life check-in and examine every aspect of yourself, paying special attention to your body. Is it trying to tell you something?

5. ***How am I doing right now with community relationships and connections?*** The Knight of Pentacles is a good worker, solid and strong. If community connections need to be made and kept, he's a good one for making that happen because he lives and works in the manifest world. If fences need mending or communications need to flow between people, take a moment and consider how to accomplish it.

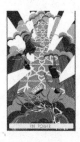

August

THE FULL MOON

When I think about the full moon in August, which is sometimes called the "Sturgeon Moon," I wonder why we call it that. Why fish, and why sturgeon, of all things? I've never been much of a fisherperson, or even a fish person for that matter, which might be a bit strange since I'm a Pisces. I respect the salmon, and when I was a kid I learned to fish for rainbow trout. But to be honest, the only seafood I enjoy to this day is actually not a fish at all, but crab. Dungeness crab meat is a treat and a delicacy where I'm from, whether it's served already picked on a bed of garlic noodles in a North Beach restaurant, or whether you pick it yourself from a cracked crab shared with family or friends. It's a mainstay for winter holiday dinners at our house, accompanied by a crisp green salad, warm sourdough French bread with slabs of butter, and an abundance of Chardonnay. There's something indulgent about a seafood dinner, something special and festive, whether it's at the holidays or another celebration.

In *Pride and Prejudice*, upon learning that Jane's wealthy, sought-after beau might be coming for dinner that evening, Mrs. Bennet bemoans the fact that there's "not a bit of fish to be got, oh, Lord!" Poor Mrs. Bennet . . . A lack of fish for dinner turned out to be the least of her worries as the story unfolded, but it gives us an insight into what was most desirable when trying to make an impression. Fish represent abundance and wealth in many societies across the world of course, not just in fussy English Regency dining rooms. They symbolize an endless river of safety and security for one's nearest and dearest in the form of a constant and stable food supply. Fish can also represent employment, honest work, and developing a lifelong understanding of natural forces well beyond human control. Knowing and respecting the sea is imperative if one is going to survive upon it, let alone make a living plumbing its depths.

The richness of the world around us is apparent in crops in the field, fish in the stream, fruit in the trees and on the vine, and the warmth we can experience with our friends and families if we're able to take some time off to relax. In August in the Northern Hemisphere the heat is on, and it's time to start thinking about the changes to come. Wherever we are, though, we can take this time to direct our energy into whatever projects and plans we have going that we want to get settled before the end of the year. We may feel like we're running out of time to get things done— summer vacations are almost over, school starts up soon, the fiscal year ends in September (at least in the United States), and planning for the holidays is just around the corner. Or perhaps none of these themes apply directly to you but you feel a sense of urgency anyway, a need to take advantage of what's present around you now that might not last, those opportunities that seem to bubble up to the surface like koi in a pond looking for a snack from a passerby with crackers.

The Full Moon—Southern Hemisphere

This is an excellent time to begin planning for your next harvest. Where do you want to be in six months? What do you want to have accomplished by then? You can start making little steps toward those goals now, or at least begin getting them mapped out for further action. What do your resources look like now that winter is almost over? How will you plan for the growing, expanding seasons to come?

THE DARK MOON

The dark moon of August is one of those occasions during the year when you can take the time to look without flinching at your failings [insert spooky voice here] *if you dare*. Given how full of possibility and expansion August's full moon is, it makes sense that the dark moon would be ripe with opportunities to let our inner demons go on a rampage in a variety of different ways. If you're not used to doing any kind of shadow work, this would be a good time to begin to approach it. If you are as familiar with your shadow as you are with old friends, this dark moon provides ample time and space to explore it more fully and unearth more layers of yourself. Just as full moons expand, dark moons contract and we draw our energies inward. Do you do so in a compassionate way, or do you find yourself getting angry and protective in a sharp way? Where do you lash out, and why? Are you not carrying your share of the load, especially with regard to community projects that need to get done on time to be of service to everybody? Or are you being a Group Project Egomaniac, taking responsibility that isn't yours and making everybody else aware of how much you're giving and how lucky they are to be working with you? Now don't get me wrong about this. There's nothing wrong with being a strong manager, leader, or commander, especially if you're female presenting. We get all kinds of signals all the time about how the better part of valor is in doing all the work and carrying the load ourselves, so it only makes sense if we don't trust that others will do their part when it comes down to it. But the shadow piece of this response grows when we don't share responsibility, when we don't allow others to do what they're supposed to do and learn their lessons when they don't. The shadow piece grows when we take over and then resent everybody else involved when we start feeling like we have to do everything ourselves. That's the thin line this demon walks, so now is a good time to walk alongside that energy and talk to it a little bit, to see if we can figure out what's what.

The Dark Moon—Southern Hemisphere

What are you carrying for others that they need to step up and start carrying for themselves? We've all got our own lives and our own burdens to carry, no matter what time of year it is or where on the globe we live, but as the winter begins to shift to spring and energies begin to loosen up and move more, it's a good time to look around and see if you've picked up anything that isn't yours that needs to be returned to its rightful owner in this time of contraction and reevaluation.

AUGUST FULL MOON

Keywords
Accumulation, multitudes, wealth, preparation

Questions to Ponder
Consider the following as you shuffle your deck. What do we need to focus on most right now? How can we best take advantage of the energies of abundance and wealth in our lives? Where are we holding ourselves back from truly appreciating what we have? Where are we allowing ourselves to be distracted from the work at hand, and why is that? Can we name all the sources of energy and flow in our lives and express gratitude for them all? Are we ready for what's to come?

Let's try to think several steps ahead now. What needs to get done? Are we forgetting anything? Breaking tasks down into detailed steps, let's examine the project that might seem overwhelming. How can we reframe it so that it's doable? We should think about our allies and our enemies—not necessarily in terms of actual people but as habits. Are we spending too much time doom-scrolling or binge-watching TV shows on a streaming service? Maybe we've all done that from time to time, so don't judge, but still: we should consider how we can gently but firmly disconnect and redirect our focus toward our goals. What brings the money in? Let's focus on that. If you're anything like me, you loathe updating your resume or CV, but it's a thing we have to do to make sure we're ready to grab the brass ring when it comes around again. As much as the Sturgeon Moon is about abundance, it's also about being a grown-up and doing what we need to do to take advantage of the abundant flow of life all around us, and to increase it for the benefit of everyone in our own circles of influence and beyond.

Spread

After shuffling, draw four cards and lay them out according to the following diagram.

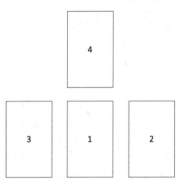

Positions

1. ***What am I not seeing that could help me take advantage of this abundant time?*** Where are my blind spots? There is value in checking in once in a while about what we're not seeing that can help us and what we're not seeing that can hurt us, especially when we're working to expand our resource base.

2. ***Where am I getting in my own way?*** Am I overthinking things? Or am I maybe not planning enough? Am I focusing so hard on the work right in front of me that I'm missing the big picture? Or is the opposite true? What damage am I doing that I can definitely stop? Sometimes we need time to work through damaging patterns, and sometimes we need to pull ourselves up short and stop the damaging behavior.

3. *What am I forgetting?* The older I get the more important this question becomes. It isn't that my to-do list isn't intimidating enough already; this question is more about remembering what's essential in any task. What's the core of what I'm doing? Have I forgotten why I'm here or what this project is really all about?

4. *Where do I need to be more of a grown-up to handle what needs doing?* There are times in life when we have to just do what needs to be done. We may not like it, we may not want to do it, we may get really annoyed at the imposition it places on our lives (whatever "it" is, like preparing and filing our taxes, for example, or making a mandatory court appearance), but the consequences of pretending the requirement doesn't exist are greater than they are if we just cowgirl up and deal with it. Much greater, perhaps. So this card will help us see where we need to face what needs facing and do what needs doing.

Sample Reading

When we look at this spread, there seems to be a lot of balancing (or attempting to establish and maintain balance) going on. There's the figure at the top, in the 2 of Pentacles card, leaping and balancing two golden disks, and the rising Angel calling the dead forth from their graves in a moment of awakening that seems both organized and a bit chaotic. Then we have the pope figure right in the middle, sitting solid in instruction and benediction, and the solo dancer in the card next to him caught mid-leap with an arc of nine cups above him, neither one moving a muscle. Solidity and fluidity are themes here, movement and stillness. And while we have fairly bright colors all over the place, we do have the ghostly figures of the dead emerging out of shadow into the light brought by the Angel—we cannot know what they have experienced in death, but we believe that emergence is at the end of it, and that gives us hope.

1. *What am I not seeing that could help me take advantage of this abundant time?* The Hierophant tells us in no uncertain terms to stop trying to reinvent the wheel. There are experts, helpers, and wisdom keepers who know what's what and who would be willing to help, or to be paid to help. They know what questions to ask, and they understand the milieu we're trying to move in.

2. *Where am I getting in my own way?* The 9 of Cups says that our desires and wishes are getting in the way of seeing clearly. We need to start seeing more with our minds and less with our hearts. Are we seeing what's really there, or only what we wish were there?

3. *What am I forgetting?* The Judgment card reminds us of what we're forgetting. What's the plan? Or more to the point, what *was* the plan before we changed it? What

are the rules and regulations that need to be followed, and which ones can be broken because they no longer apply?

4. *Where do I need to be more of a grown-up to handle what needs doing?* The 2 of Pentacles shows us that being a grown-up means juggling priorities, navigating treacherous waters, and dancing for our lives. Life is hard and challenging, but there are good parts too. It's ok to enjoy the dance as we go.

AUGUST DARK MOON

Keywords
Overwhelm, burdens, anxiety, theft

Questions to Ponder
Consider the following as you shuffle your deck. Where are we letting things slide? Where are we letting other people get away with murder because we don't want to stand up and tell them to start carrying their fair share? What martyr mask are we wearing, and more importantly, how do we take it off without hurting ourselves or anyone around us? Are we overwhelmed and feeling so out of our depth that we can't see our way forward? Are we taking it out on others? How do we change that behavior?

Let's think about contraction, about the reduction of resources when there's still just as much work to be done. About what makes us angry or sad, overwhelmed or exhausted. About what still needs to happen as the summer is winding down. Perhaps vacations are ending. Maybe change is looming, and we don't feel like there's enough time to get ready.

Spread
After shuffling, draw four cards and lay them out according to the following diagram.

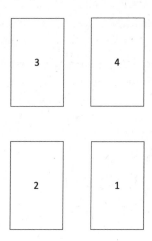

Positions

1. *How is my shadow side manifesting right now?*
   Sometimes we are the last people to see how we are engaging with the world, and it can help to have a mirror held up to show us what we're doing. What's different between how we speak to others and how we speak to ourselves? Be honest about what's coming up.

2. *Where am I letting my shadow side run rampant?* Think back to the description of the Group Project Egomaniac. Are you running roughshod over everybody else's ideas and opinions? Is yours the only voice being heard? Are you centering your own needs in an unhealthy or unkind way that feels unjustified? Is your give-and-take meter out of balance?

3. *How can I work with that energy in a positive way?* Rather than giving yourself endless grief about the challenging information being brought up, how can you reframe it so that it's just information and not a personal failing? Even if it *feels* like a personal failing, is there a

way you can release that feeling and just focus on the data you're receiving?

4. *What are my demons trying to teach me right now?* What's the lesson in all this? It can be different for everyone, so don't worry too much about how other people solve their problems if it doesn't work for you; find your own way through. What's the value your demons can bring to you, the treasure you find when you face your shadow without blinking?

Sample Reading

When we look at the cards all together, only one looks like it might fit the description of a "shadow" card, and that's the 10 of Swords. It's a hard card for some because it looks like wall-to-wall drama in the style of a horror movie. The flock of black birds above the swords would be enough to curdle anyone's blood, but the rest of the cards show what in other contexts would be comfort, joy, and good work. So what's going on here? We've got two 10s in this reading, and two court cards from the suit of Pentacles (Earth). There are no Major Arcana cards showing up, so the energies are perhaps easier and friendlier to work with—less "life and death" intensity and more "dealing with the business of living" vibes. That doesn't mean the messages aren't as important, though, as we will see.

1. *How is my shadow side manifesting right now?* The 10 of Cups says that perhaps a desire to show others only goodness or happiness is inauthentic to our actual experience. There is stagecraft here. Are we being dishonest with those around us?

2. *Where am I letting my shadow side run rampant?* The Page of Pentacles is so eager to help, but the desire to be useful is getting in the way of actually getting the job done. Slow down, back up, listen, and get help.

3. *How can I work with that energy in a positive way?*
The 10 of Swords says that we cannot work with this energy in a positive way except by leaving it alone. What's needed right now is to acknowledge the truth of what is and then let it go.

4. *What are my demons trying to teach me right now?*
The Queen of Pentacles brings this message: It's ok if the garden is a little overgrown. It's ok if everything gets a bit hoary and long-fingered. Let it be. Everything will get taken care of in time, even ourselves.

QUEEN OF PENTACLES

PAGE OF PENTACLES

September

THE FULL MOON

September is a time of both beginnings and endings in the Northern Hemisphere. Traditional school systems are getting into the swing of the school year, new friendships are made, new plans are developing, and even the Autumnal Equinox happens in September. Several of my friends have wedding anniversaries in September, which makes me think of new lives and new families all starting fresh in the golden autumn fields near my home. September is a period of endings as well, because it's a harvest season for plants of all kinds. There are companies whose fiscal year ends at the end of September, perhaps as a nod to the English festival of Michaelmas on September 29, which traditionally marked the time by which harvests had to be in and rents were due. This created an energy of ferocious doing in September that English settlers brought with them when they colonized much of the Western world. If we live in an agricultural community, the process of harvesting and preparing for winter has an edge of intensity that might not be familiar to those of us for whom the word "agriculture" means the produce section of our local market. But no matter where we live in the Northern Hemisphere or how, there is no escaping the changing quality of the light, the shortening of the days that is just beginning to be noticeable. Perhaps there are moments when you can sense the coming change, the turn of the Great Wheel just across the horizon that will bring a new season and, with it, new blessings and challenges.

The full moon of September is one of Mother Nature's greatest "impossible to miss" reminders that we need to make sure we're in step with Her as winter approaches, because life moves at a great clip. Sometimes called the "Corn Moon," when it hangs full in the sky and takes on the beautiful orange sheen from reflected sunlight, it's an opportunity to joyfully notice how we can flow with the changes coming to us. It can be an exciting time of new work and new enthusiasm we are invited to share with friends and neighbors alike. It's the last full moon of the summer, and amidst its energy, there is a feeling that we are being watched over as we begin our push toward the end of the year. We are reminded of community in this time of climate change, when hurricanes rage and wildfires explode across dry countryside during these late summer days. Community that used to work in harmony to bring in crops far and wide, so that everyone was ready for the coming darkness, now works to shield and shelter one another from environmental disasters, or to assist wherever possible so that schools and businesses can function with as much normalcy as possible. We not only harvest our own fields (literally or metaphorically), but we also remember that we are all relatives of one another. Doing what we can for people around us, whether we know them or not, is part of this full moon's call.

The Full Moon—Southern Hemisphere

Even though it's not the end of summer like it is up north, it still is a liminal time of endings and beginnings, and you can tap into that energy. Where can you summon the energy you need to get ready for what's next? Do you need to gather resources for the changes to come? Perhaps the requirements aren't quite as obvious as getting the corn harvest in before the cold comes, or maybe they are. What is the equivalent for you? How can you harvest what you need in order to be ready when change happens?

THE DARK MOON

As big as the September full moon is, the energy of this month's dark moon is small, restrictive, a contraction of all those big energies, as if a rubber band has snapped back hard from being over-stretched. We push so hard to open up, and work even harder to do everything that needs to get done, and then the energies of the dark moon pull it all back in on us, possibly bringing up feelings of lack, resentment, and needing to turn away from everything that isn't the self. Dark moons are a perfect time to reset boundaries and reevaluate commitments, and it's valuable to note that in September the dark moon's energy can tend toward selfishness and self-absorption, which might even lead to a grim determination to reject connection and community ties that we previously worked so hard to develop.

If you consider this in the context of the harvest metaphor, it makes sense. We're doing everything we can to prepare ourselves for future deprivation and need, and we're working hard to get tasks and projects done that will serve us and our communities going forward. Sharing the fruits of our labor with others can feed this energy of resentment if the sharing isn't couched properly in terms of group service that works for the benefit of everyone, *including us.* If that's not clear, of course we're going to feel like we're the only ones working hard and everybody else is just Miss Slackery Slackington of Slackertown. Facing that tendency with honesty can help us understand why we feel this way and how we can fix it, or at least speak to it so that it doesn't overwhelm us. We can examine our shadow tendencies before they stop us from working with others, and we can try to find ways to nurture ourselves enough so that it never feels like working in community means depriving ourselves.

The Dark Moon—Southern Hemisphere

You wouldn't be alone if you were to say you're exhausted and depleted right now but are unclear on how to fix it. Even though the dark season of the year is approaching in the north, for you it's retreating and the time of light and energy is at hand, which may be exhausting just to think about. Do you find yourself retreating and relying on boundaries to shield you in these times? Are you not showing up, for whatever reason, and making excuses about it? How are you working with your shadow energy right now?

SEPTEMBER FULL MOON

Keywords
Harvest, work, intensity, bounty

Questions to Ponder
Consider the following as you shuffle your deck. Think about community and obligations, what needs to get done versus what we want to happen, because they're not always the same things. Let's take some time to consider where we are on the helper spectrum: Do we try to do everything ourselves because we don't trust others to carry their share of the load (I'm looking at myself here and trying not to project)? Do we focus so much on helping others that we don't get our own work done and end up in an endless cycle of struggle? The September full moon is a time of harvesting in a very real, material sense—not the "just getting started" sense of Lammas last month or the "ancestral soul harvest" sense of Samhain next month. This is the time of year when harvesting means supplies, resources, support, and getting everything ready for lean times ahead. Let's think about what that means in our lives, and how we can work with that energy now, either in our own gardens or fields or in a different way in our homes, schools, or workplaces.

Spread
After shuffling, draw six cards and lay them out according to the following diagram.

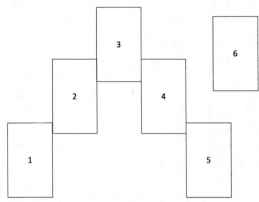

Positions

1. ***What needs to get done more than anything else right now?*** Sometimes when we have a monstrous to-do list we focus on the easiest things to do first, just to get them out of the way and to satisfy ourselves that we're doing *something*. Or maybe that's just me. This card will help us see where we need to be putting our focus, so that instead of staring at a whole field of corn wondering where on earth to begin harvesting, we can pick one stalk, the most urgently waving stalk, the one jumping up and down yelling, "Me, me, me first!" and start there.

2. ***What has been forgotten that's long past due?*** Thank heavens most libraries have stopped charging for overdue books, because if they still did and I was still in school, well, let's just say I'd be in debt to the county library system big time. I just can't read as fast as I used to, sadly, and it seems like the number of distractions grows as I age. But this card will help us pinpoint anything that we've forgotten about that needs to be handled as a part of this month's harvest moon so that we can take care of

it and not keep carrying it forward with increasing debt and worry.

3. *How can I engage with the community and share the workload so that we all make it across the finish line together?* This is basically another way of asking, "How can I help?" If we have privilege in our communities, helping is something we need to be doing all across the board. It doesn't have to be about money if you don't have money, and it doesn't have to be about time if you don't have time. This card will help us see how we can reach out to community to produce real assistance to the most folks who need help, with the aim of bringing us all forward together—not just putting Band-Aids on open veins, but finding ways to close the wounds from without and within so that the community body heals in whatever way it needs to.

4. *What are we not seeing that can help us?* My friend Anastasia is very fond of using her cards to ask this question, and I think it's genius. While we're so focused on doing the work we need to do to get the job done, to provide assistance, to complete projects and update plans, let's take a quick glance into our blind spots. What are we missing that can make our work easier and our lives better?

5. *What can we do right now to prepare for what's to come?* This card can help us see next steps. Granted, once I'm done with a big job it's pretty much pajama-pants-and-Netflix time, but here we're reminded to not let go just yet. What do we need to do to tie up loose ends and make sure we're ready for whatever's up ahead?

6. *What is the harvest gift for us?* This is a nice way to look at what's around us and see our gifts; it's a "count your

blessings" reminder that also can help us find gifts and blessings where we least expect them.

Sample Reading

So here we have a multitude of information, taking a quick glance at the cards as a pattern unto themselves. Two Major Arcana cards give weight to the reading; three cards with multiple figures and three with solitary figures suggest balance between self and community; and an Ace and the Death card give us both beginnings and endings, which is fitting for September. While there are no Sword cards in this reading, we can infer the Air element from the Hermit's stance before the full moon itself. It's worth noting that the main element represented in the reading is the Fire of the Wands suit—the golden light of the Wands exists in every card: casting a reflection on the figures in darkness in the 5 of Pentacles, in the ribbon of light along the eternal far shore beyond the river of the dead and dying in the Death card, in the great moon of the Hermit card, in the wands of both the Ace and 6 of Wands cards, and in the golden cups above and below the figure in the 4 of Cups card. This light, this fire, is present no matter what we do this month. Our passion is the key.

1. *What needs to get done more than anything else right now?* The 5 of Pentacles speaks of poverty consciousness, fear, and literally missing out on the answer to our prayers because our focus is so intent on the pain and suffering of the situation that we're blind to the fact that help and shelter are immediately available. We are being invited not only to think positive, but to think fierce, ferocious, and alive!

2. *What has been forgotten that's long past due?* Death. We're all going to die. Death is a natural part of life. The corn dies so that we might live. If we eat animals, they die

so that we can survive. Remember that we are all moving toward an end and whatever lies beyond it.

3. ***How can I engage with the community and share the workload so that we all make it across the finish line together?*** The Hermit is about going it solo, going within and facing whatever needs facing alone. If we think about community needs in regards to the Hermit, the idea comes up that we as individuals have work to do in order to be useful to community. The Hermit is telling us to do our work and ask ourselves the hard questions so that we can be useful members of a more just society for everyone.

4. ***What are we not seeing that can help us?*** The Ace of Wands, the fire of ideas and planning, is inviting us to see any question we're facing in a new way and providing us the possibility of resources as we do so. We have the key within us.

5. ***What can we do right now to prepare for what's to come?*** The 6 of Wands is giving us some ideas for how to

proceed. "Fake it 'til you make it" and maybe even "Crown yourself, queen!" is the wisdom the card provides if we interpret it as a direct answer to the question. It's always wise to plan ahead for success, because those plans will see us through the dark times when it feels like hope for success is lost.

6. *What is the harvest gift for us?* The 4 of Cups is often thought of as the "divine discontent" card. We're bored, we're tired, we're up to here with things as they are, and we're not sure how to go about getting the change we want. The 4 of Cups is reminding us to open up to miracles.

SEPTEMBER DARK MOON

Keywords
Rejection, self-righteousness, boundaries, narrowness

Questions to Ponder
Consider the following as you shuffle your deck. In what ways are we allowing feelings of self-righteousness and judgment of others to take over in our community work? When we engage in service to others, how are we *really* showing up? Is it a virtue-signaling opportunity—a "look at me!" kind of thing? Where do we let appearances be enough rather than digging in and making a good-faith effort to do the work? When the dark-moon energies encourage contracting, do we allow ourselves to retreat and refresh, or do we fight the boundaries and the natural flow?

Spread
After shuffling, draw four cards and lay them out according to the following diagram.

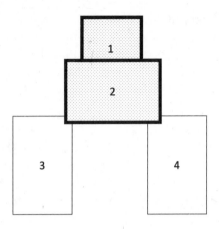

Positions

1. *How do I* think *I show up in service to others?* Do I see myself as a savior, a martyr to the cause? Am I the one who always brings food, the nurturer? Do I see myself as the peacemaker, the wise one with all the answers, the worker bee who always does everything? Recognizing how we see ourselves can be very valuable when trying to figure out if we're causing problems or bringing loads of baggage with us without realizing it.

2. *How do I* actually *show up in service to others?* We know where this is going, right? We think we're the peacemaker, but we actually bring more fractious energy with us than we ever resolve. We think we're the nurturer, but we're really the wounded child who needs more TLC than we provide. What attributes do we bring with us most strongly when we engage with community, and where can we work to make that energy more positive?

3. *In what ways am I allowing my shadow self to replace true service to the community with self-righteousness?* We all do it, right? Where do we puff ourselves up instead of focusing on the work at hand? This isn't

about judgment, by the way; it's an attempt to recognize where motivations get in the way of actually helping. If we follow our shadow inclinations, we might end up creating or supporting false solutions instead of listening to those whose experiences and opinions speak directly to what we're trying to fix. How can we identify when we're coming from shadow energy so that we can stop ourselves from creating harm?

4. *What does my shadow most want to bring to my conscious mind right now?* If our shadow selves could speak, what would they say and what could we learn from them?

Sample Reading

There's so much going on in these cards that it might be a challenge to get settled with what we're seeing. There are Swords in two cards, Cups in one, and Wands in one. No Pentacles (Earth). No Major Arcana. So these cards are going to speak about internal processes and how we reflect ourselves from the inside out. In two cards there are solitary figures and in two we have a small group, indicating intimacy and working closely with ourselves and others. And the themes represented lean more toward the day-to-day processes of living rather than the Big Issues so often represented in the Major Arcana. We won't have to look too far for answers here.

1. *How do I* think *I show up in service to others?* The 2 of Cups is a card often associated with marriage, harmony, and right relationship between us and the world. Who wouldn't want to show up this way? But this can be problematic if we see the world as we want to see it rather than as it really is, and in any relationship that can be dangerous. Make sure that what you're looking at and what you're seeing are the same thing.

2. *How do I* actually *show up in service to others?* The 8 of Swords brings the light of truth to how we really show up in service to others. We are a great deal less confident in ourselves and our abilities than we think we are, or than we want others to think we are. The 8 of Swords can also be read as a card of initiation and practice, so maybe we think we're not ready to be out there with the Big Kids yet.

3. *In what ways am I allowing my shadow self to replace true service to the community with self-righteousness?* The 6 of Swords is a bit of a puzzle at first glance. How can fleeing the field of play and moving beyond where we are at the moment be considered self-righteous? Maybe there are ways of considering our options that can take into account both what we want out of life and what we have to offer before doing something like choosing not to play at all, which in the long run serves no one. Is there a temptation within ourselves to "take our resources and go home" if our help (the way *we* see it as being given) isn't immediately accepted and praised, rather than giving regardless of how the gift is used? We'd do well to remember that those most affected are in the best position to know what's needed most.

4. *What does my shadow most want to bring to my conscious mind right now?* The 7 of Wands. If our shadow self wants to be a fighter, so be it, but maybe it's more helpful to look at how being aggressive or passive-aggressive isn't what's useful. Maybe there are ways to let go of some of the things to be upset about in the world and just focus instead on the ones we can bring positive change to.

Autumnal Equinox

Keywords
Balance, equality, fire, control

More than a few couples I know have gotten married on or around the Autumnal Equinox, a wonderful time to have a wedding around here. While other places may celebrate weddings in early summer, where I live the early and midsummer days are swathed in fog that's so pervasive and such a force of nature that it's actually got its own Twitter account. Climate change is now affecting Karl (our name for the fog) just as it's affecting everything else. Still, the late summer and early autumn days are true summer around here. The Great Wheel turns and we move from sweaters, blankets at baseball games, and maybe seeing fireworks on the Fourth of July depending on the fog layer, to wildfire season, watching the skies uneasily for shifting winds and smoke, carrying N95 masks for non-Covid reasons, and still celebrating weddings and birthdays out in the beautiful landscape that's just beginning to turn toward the chill of the final harvest. It's not usually until the Autumnal Equinox that we find ourselves celebrating summer and finding ways to enjoy all it means.

The Autumnal Equinox is also a good time to review our personal harvests. We are at a tipping point between expending and conserving energy, moving from high activity toward introspection as the light eventually fades and we approach the season of the dead.

Questions to Ponder
Consider the following as you shuffle your deck. At the equinoxes, day and night are equal length. It's a perfect time to consider how balanced our lives are at the moment. During the last few years, with the pandemic and political upheaval, with all kinds

of patriarchal and colonialist horrors making themselves not only known but obvious in our society, it might be a particularly grueling challenge to find balance, or even to remember what balance felt like before these crises exploded on so many levels all at once. Still, it's important to ask ourselves where we can find balance or build it into our lives at this moment of pivoting, to check in with the plans and ideas we "planted" during the Spring Equinox and see how those are proceeding. Let's take a look at the presence of fire in our lives and how it manifests both literally and figuratively. Have we ever had to deal with a conflagration? Or has fire been more of a comforting presence in our lives, as a provider of a boundary and barrier against the anxiety and fear that the darkness can bring?

Southern Hemisphere

You might be moving from the hot season into rainy weather, or from the darkness of winter into more light. But it's still a good time to question how you manage balance in your life and where the elements are out of control. If it's the beginning of the planting season rather than harvest time, you can think about what plans and projects you want to grow and develop in the months to come and how you can use the turning-point energy of this time to change gears and begin to put your ideas into effect.

Spread

After shuffling, draw six cards and lay them out according to the following diagram.

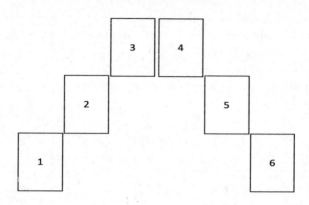

Positions

1. *How are the seeds that I planted six months ago doing?* This is a good time to do a spot check to see how things are progressing with our plans, what's gone awry, what's just sitting there, and what really doesn't suit us anymore the way we thought it would.

2. *What's ready to be acted on (or "harvested")?* What's ready to go? Are we sitting on any projects and not taking action to complete them for any reason? Is there something we need to face about getting things over the finish line?

3. *What shifts can I make now to take fuller advantage of my harvest?* This is a good time to take a look at how we sabotage ourselves (if that's a thing for us), how we procrastinate or dawdle, and what steps we can take to help ourselves finish what needs finishing.

4. *What's my relationship with balance like at the moment?* I don't know anyone who is currently fully in balance with life. This card in this position will allow us to take a look at what we might already know: how we

prioritize balance and what we can do to improve that relationship.

5. *What's on fire in my life that I'm unaware of?* Let's take a look at those problem areas and see if we can stop a conflagration before it starts.

6. *What's one step I can take right now to help me celebrate my harvest?* This may seem like a no-brainer, but some of us need an assist when it comes to party planning. My sister was a genius at it, but I definitely didn't get that gene, so things that come very easily to some folks—like inviting friends over for dinner or planning a picnic or beach trip or mountain getaway—are very often ordeals for me. So like the true Tarot nerd I am, I pull cards to give me ideas on how to have fun after the work is done.

Sample Reading

The Autumnal Equinox draw seems to be offering us an excellent opportunity to figure things out on our own. Given how much this spread delves into our personal relationships with several different themes, it makes sense that community, crowds, even family either are not present here or are considered on a meta level rather than in a concrete sense. There's lots of light and clear skies in the cards, telling us that maybe things are clearer than we think they are and that we should watch out for instances in which we might be making things harder on ourselves than they have to be. We also have two Major Arcana cards, which indicate success and show tons of light, both in the daytime (the Sun) and at night (the Chariot), which makes sense for this time of year. And Cups is the only suit not represented, perhaps leading us to believe that the emotional undercurrents of our lives won't be part of the discussion—although the shades of blue in five of the six cards show us that those emotional, unseen, watery undercurrents will be doing their undercurrent-y thing the whole time while the elements of Air, Fire, and Earth manage the conscious conversation.

1. *How are the seeds that I planted six months ago doing?* The Chariot. That's heartening! Things are moving forward pretty well it seems, and we've gotten ourselves to a place where we can make changes and pivot without too much drama or hard work to enforce our adjustments.

2. *What's ready to be acted on (or "harvested")?* The Knight of Wands represents movement, passion, and high energy. Turning this focus onto our fields of endeavor to see what's ready to be harvested, we are advised to look at what we're most passionate about, what we want to jump in and handle right now.

3. *What shifts can I make now to take fuller advantage of my harvest?* The Sun tells us to move. Do. Stop procrastinating and do whatever you need to do to get the job done. Not everything comes with instructions, and sometimes we have to just figure it out. This is one of those times. Have faith and take action.

4. *What's my relationship with balance like at the moment?* The 4 of Pentacles reminds us that sitting absolutely still isn't actually balance. Balance requires action, movement, and again, faith—faith that we won't fall over, hurt ourselves, hurt someone else, or be a colossal failure.

5. *What's on fire in my life that I'm unaware of?* The 2 of Wands is often associated with dominion over the earth, but if we start thinking about how this might be "on fire," what comes up might be something about the status of the earth itself—perhaps regarding climate change, politics, war, or any of the other forces pushing change all around us.

6. ***What's one step I can take right now to help me celebrate my harvest?*** The 2 of Swords. Thought and desire are in balance here, and that's what's needed for celebration: we acknowledge the emotional reality of the situation, positive or negative, and we recognize what has to be cut, removed, "harvested" when the time is right.

October

THE FULL MOON

October is one of my favorite months of the year. The light begins to shimmer, and I can feel the end of the calendar year approaching. Yule is on the horizon, and after weeks of hot weather, the approach of winter and the slightest possibility of rain, even of cloudy days, brings me joy. I search weather almanacs to determine whether it's an El Niño or La Niña year, and I join 40 million other Californians up and down the state as we pray for rain. When I was a kid, wildfires were rare events, certainly not the monthly or even weekly occurrences they are now. These are the days of climate change, though, so October is the month when the skies might be so thick and dark with wildfire smoke that it wouldn't really be a surprise to see Sauron's armies marching down my street as if it were the Morgul Vale at the end of *The Lord of the Rings*. But regardless of the unyielding smoke and the fear or reality of wildfire, October is when the end-of-the-year energies begin to buzz for me, when days are short and the harvest moon hangs so low in the sky I feel like I could close my eyes and reach out and touch it.

October's full moon is sometimes called the "Hunter's Moon," giving us the dramatic image of hunter and prey going through their life-and-death chase out in the natural world before the onset of winter makes hunting difficult. Maybe hunting is a common activity where you live, or maybe the hunter-prey interaction exists mainly among insects, birds, fish, and other animals where you are. Or you may live in an urban or metro-suburban setting like me, where hunting doesn't happen beyond someone's backyard or patio garden, unless a coyote is seen running through the streets at night, or perhaps a mountain lion is caught on security camera footage padding from backyard to backyard looking for small animals left outside. While we can go to a market with relative ease these days to get the meat, fish, and produce we want, the change of seasons carries a reminder that no matter how convenient things are, we remain only one or two catastrophes away from winter being a life-or-death event. Our recent experience with global disease should have taught us that. Life is always at stake.

The Full Moon—Southern Hemisphere
Is the growing season beginning where you are? How can you ground your energies and purpose with the serious focus you'll be grateful for later, while still hanging on to the lightness and playful vibes of this time of year? Are the plants blossoming and babies being born? Is it the time when the rains start? Is the sun rising higher in the desert? How can you tune into the voices of your ancestors as they whisper through the changing land around you?

THE DARK MOON
October in much of the Western world means Halloween, and Halloween means costumes and masks, hiding who we really are in order to let ourselves be someone or something else for a night. It's probably a surprise to literally no one that my favorite Halloween costume when I was a kid was a fortune-teller. I loved the rich fabrics and bright colors, the swirling skirts, the bangles and beads, and letting myself be as dramatic as my little Pisces heart wanted to be. I don't think I ever actually gave anyone any fortunes, and I didn't use cards or a crystal ball as props—that wasn't going to happen with my parents around, since they couldn't abide even the word "occult," much less items that could easily be a witch's trademark—but I got to step into the world of mystery and spirit in a way that spoke to me, even though I wouldn't understand the languages of divination until much later. This is the magic of Halloween for us. It's a candy holiday, sure, and without it we probably wouldn't ever have known what Necco Wafers are, or Smarties, or the joy of getting some actual

chocolate in your haul of mostly Charleston Chews, Sugar Babies, Pop Rocks, and Pez. But part of the fun was in being mysterious, in hiding, in setting aside the regular world to dream up something new in the dark.

There is of course a downside to this, and I experienced that as well. In a testament to just how much we could get away with in high school in the 1980s, when I was seventeen I went to a Halloween dance dressed as a guerilla soldier. I was angry that no one had asked me to the dance, so I dressed up in my father's military fatigues, pulled on a ski mask, and even carried a toy gun to the event. I skulked around and menaced people, watched them dance, and made snide, bitter remarks until I eventually went home and probably cried—because of course the anger was never just about not being asked to the dance. It was about being seventeen and frustrated, exasperated, and disappointed, and acting out in this negative way was my first foray into poisoning myself as a way of getting back at others. Leaving aside any "cry for help" commentary and acknowledging the *breathtaking* white privilege that allowed me to even dream up such a thing—let alone actually do it—it's an example of what can go wrong with wearing masks and costumes to act out our worst impulses instead of dealing with them appropriately. When the great Hunter's Moon of October disappears from the sky, we put on masks to hide from evil and maybe from our own selves.

The Dark Moon—Southern Hemisphere

Halloween is Halloween wherever you are, and the idea behind "trick or treat" is fairly universal: whether spring or autumn, warm or cold, a fancy-dress party or trick-or-treating up and down dark, windy streets, we wear costumes to become other than we are. What is the costuming tradition where you are? Are you from a culture that uses dress-up differently, if at all? How are these themes playing out in your life right now?

OCTOBER FULL MOON

Keywords
Preservation, foresight, preparation

Questions to Ponder
Consider the following as you shuffle your deck. For many of us, it took a global pandemic to remind us that life is an uncertain, precarious business and nothing is ever guaranteed. How well prepared are we? What steps have we taken to make sure that if anything happened to us, our family wouldn't suffer needlessly? What can we do now to make things easier and safer for ourselves and our loved ones later? What do we need to protect ourselves from, and where is our assistance and protection needed that we might not be aware of, with everything else going on at the moment?

Spread
After shuffling, draw four cards and lay them out according to the following diagram.

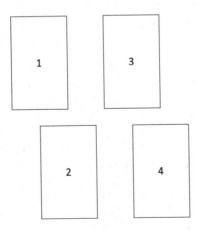

Positions

1. *What wisdom can the huge, bright moon reveal this month that I most need to gather in?* The moon is often worked with as an energy of the unconscious, the unknown, the tides of Fate that move and direct us without us knowing it. So asking what we can draw down from that unseen river during this full moon makes sense. How are we being shifted from one phase to the next? Maybe the question is as simple as "what's happening?" or "why?" Or perhaps we're working through a more complicated "if . . . then . . ." situation and could really use a bright idea from our unconscious mind. Look carefully at the card that appears here to see how the moon directs us toward what we most need going forward.

2. *How well prepared am I really for what's next?* Let this be a card of warning as to what could happen if we're not on the ball enough to prevent it—or, at the very least, to see how we can mitigate potential disaster.

3. *What can I use my magic to draw down?* Yes, we all do have magic, and we can use it to reach out and call what we need to ourselves. Keep in mind, though, that what shows up may not look like you thought it would. Be careful not to turn away something that you asked for just because it doesn't have all the bells and whistles that you think it should. And let's remember our ethics—let's call in what's ours and nothing else.

4. *How can I best protect myself and others right now?* October's energies spin and deepen after the Autumnal Equinox, and there are lots of wild things about. Others who may not be concerned with being in right relationship with the various energies of the perceived and unperceived worlds ·can do lots of damage right now (or at any time, really, but most especially when

we're near the seasonal doors of Bealtaine, Samhain, the solstices, and the equinoxes). It's always a good idea to not be around when that damage manifests, or at least to be well-shielded from it.

Sample Reading

Our draw this full moon is both balanced and poignant: along the bottom line there are cards of elemental Earth (Pentacles) representing the world made manifest, while above them are the Hierophant, representing ultimate spiritual authority in the world, and two children playing, bringing a flow of sweetness and emotional sensitivity. The children above and the two figures in the 5 of Pentacles below show the most vulnerable members of society, while the Hierophant is easily among the least vulnerable. There is grown-up power and understanding contrasted with childhood expression, and abject poverty contrasted with the source of all wealth and material resources. We don't see any Wands or Swords here, so we may have to delve a bit to get to the Fire and Air wisdom this full moon spread has for us; but the Hierophant himself draws in both passion and wisdom, so that shouldn't be too challenging.

1. ***What wisdom can the huge, bright moon reveal this month that I most need to gather in?*** The Hierophant can be energetically activating in negative ways because of everything it implies about patriarchy, imperialism, colonialism, and literally a millennium and a half of misuse of spiritual authority for temporal gain. The teachings of the Christian church, though, are rooted in service to the poor, the sick, and the helpless who need protection. The Hierophant helps us see that taking our place as responsible community leaders who are grounded in ethics—and being in right relationship with ourselves, community, and the world—is key.

2. *How well prepared am I really for what's next?* The 5 of Pentacles is just about the loudest "YOU'RE NOT READY" card there is in the deck (except maybe the Tower), and there's a sort of warning going on here: no matter what happens, keep moving, keep your wits, and if you can, keep your sense of humor.

3. *What can I use my magic to draw down?* The 6 of Cups tells us to get help. Rely on friends and trusted allies. Lean on your people, your team, your squad. Let them lean on you as well.

4. *How can I best protect myself and others right now?* The Ace of Pentacles tells us that we need to make our protection real-world real. It's not enough to just think about it or plan to do it. We are being called on to create a plan to protect whatever we have to protect in actuality

and then do it—lock those doors (or add a deadbolt lock), remember to close and lock windows when leaving the house, put your purse or wallet into a locked drawer at work, keep your phone in an RFID-blocking pouch, and keep your money in a bank or credit union. Take the threats of the world around you seriously, no matter how small.

OCTOBER DARK MOON

Keywords
Masks, costumes, fear, demons, Halloween

Questions to Ponder
Consider the following as you shuffle your deck. What are our favorite costumes? What masks do we wear when push comes to shove? Do we let our angry impulses out only when we're in costume, allowing the characters we're playing to take responsibility and blame for our real feelings? Do we go to extremes to escape? Why do we pick the costumes we wear? What are we trying to communicate to others about ourselves through our masks?

Spread
After shuffling, draw four cards and lay them out according to the following diagram.

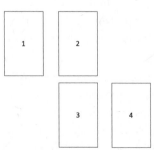

Positions

1. *What mask am I wearing right now?* Am I actually being who I am, or am I pretending to be someone or something I'm not? I saw a news story one day, some time back, about the music artist Lil Nas X and how his work and his public presentation are about authenticity and being his truest self. It made me think: Am I my truest self, or do I wear a mask I'm so used to that I've forgotten I'm even wearing it? What face do I show people? Is it real or is it my costume, my persona?

2. *What is that mask really telling others about me?* Do I think I'm compassionate while others perceive me as a pushover? Do I think I'm being honest when in fact I'm being a bully? What is my mask telling people about me that I don't know or can't see for myself, and how can I use that information to make changes for the better?

3. *How am I being hurt by not being my authentic self?* This may seem overly obvious, that being one's authentic self should be something that just comes naturally, but that's not always the case. There are times when it's simply not safe to be who we are, sadly, and there may be times when we just don't want to be authentic, for whatever reason. But it's important to identify how we're being hurt by our own refusal to be real so that we can make a more informed choice in those cases where it's safe to do so.

4. *What door am I using a mask or character to close behind me?* In other words, what ending am I so uncomfortable making that I need help making it? Sometimes pretending to be someone we're not can be useful. We might need to act in a way that's uncomfortable or new to us (for

example, making a difficult phone call, or saying "no" to someone we're not used to saying "no" to). So it's useful sometimes to put on a "success face," the persona of someone who has done to great acclaim whatever you need to do. And if you find yourself needing to wear a mask right now, it's important to take a good look at why.

Sample Reading

In this draw we see individual figures in three of the four cards, which makes sense given the questions we're asking. There is one Major Arcana card to start off with, one queen, and two Minor Arcana figures with armfuls of Swords (Air) and Wands (Fire). Note what's missing: Cups (Water) and Pentacles (Earth). We're dealing with Air and Fire with this draw, so it would be useful to ask where our heart is as we go through this, because it's not showing up in these cards. We see lots of bright light and vibrant colors in these cards, emphasizing the presence of Fire and the energy of creation it represents.

1. *What mask am I wearing right now?* The Empress. If anybody in the Tarot is large and in charge, it's the Empress. She represents female temporal power. She's not just a queen, she's the queen of queens, and that's the face we're showing the world right now.

2. *What is that mask really telling others about me?* The Queen of Wands suggests that others view us as magical because of the presence of the wand in the Queen's right hand and the movement of her swirling skirts. There is energetic flow all around her, within which she balances herself perfectly. When we embody her, we appear to others to be balanced in both affairs of the heart and work of the material world.

3. *How am I being hurt by not being my authentic self?* The 7 of Swords is a card of thievery here no matter how

you look at it: we're either stealing from others, being stolen from, or stealing from ourselves. These cards are telling us that we are stealing from ourselves by wearing the mask of the Empress, pretending to be something we're not. There is an inauthenticity about it that is hurtful to our well-being.

4. ***What door am I using a mask or character to close behind me?*** The 10 of Wands is one of those cards that is almost hilarious in its depiction of overdoing absolutely everything. I can barely get up the stairs at home with four bags of groceries, much less dance on my toes in a billowing gown while balancing ten large wands on my back. And that's the point of this card: we've gotten to a zplace where we're doing too much. There's an opportunity to start saying "no" more often and more clearly, and to stop letting the fear of others' expectations be the driver of how we are in the world.

Samhain

Keywords

Ancestors, the dead, visions, death, renewal

*H*alloween is by far the most popular and well-known of all the pagan holidays, perhaps because it's not really known or thought of as a pagan holiday. It's something people can participate in and enjoy regardless of their age or spiritual involvement (or lack thereof). Children dress up in costumes for school and town parades; people decorate their dwellings and yards with gauzy spider webs occupied by fuzzy bouncing spiders; recordings of barking hellhounds and maniacal laughter float through the air; ramshackle gravestones decorate previously pristine front steps; and maybe a Frankenstein or a zombie lurches out from behind a potted plant whenever a trick-or-treater gets too close. There are carved pumpkins lit from within, lanterns swinging in the wind, sneering vampires lounging in packs looking cool and desperate, and costume parties with a Tarot reader swathed in scarves reading fortunes for giggling teenagers. This is the secular layer of a much deeper spiritual event, and for most people that's as far as it goes.

Just because most people don't venture deeper than carving pumpkins and handing out candy doesn't mean the depths don't exist. Samhain (pronounced "SOW-inn") is the Irish name for this holiday, and the word in the Irish language literally means "first of November." Like Mexican Day of the Dead celebrations, Samhain in Ireland and elsewhere is a time of honoring the dead, remembering them, speaking to them, and telling "ghost stories" about the people who have gone before us into the Land of the Dead. Like the Day of the Dead, Samhain has become quite popular in the United States and elsewhere in the English-speaking world, perhaps because it provides a kind of structure, a modality for working with the dead that doesn't exist in many religious structures in the West. We don't know how to talk to our dead (or we're terrified of doing so), and so we consciously or unconsciously lean on Indigenous cultures who have living traditions of doing just that. Hopefully we do so without appropriation and with respect, not taking but learning, supporting, and honoring the tradition's culture of origin in any way we can. The richness and attraction of a life layered with ancestral reverence, that radiates meaning, support, and connection beyond what exists to be perceived by our mortal senses, is powerful and undeniable.

They say that Samhain and Bealtaine, at opposite sides of the Wheel, are the times of the year when the "veils" or boundaries between this world and all the others are thinnest, that these are times when spirits can move between their home plane and this one, speaking to us in ways that they can't ordinarily. I'm not sure how it all works, but I've participated in Samhain rituals that honor and celebrate the dead, that literally focus so powerfully and completely on the dead that if my great-grandmother who died in early twentieth-century San Francisco had plopped down beside me and said hello, I wouldn't have been even a little bit surprised. Establishing and welcoming that level of connection with our ancestors during Samhain is the point, or at least part of the point; the rest depends on how you celebrate, where you live, and what your traditions are. Some witches celebrate the New Year at Samhain, turning over the Wheel of the old year into the liminal space between Samhain and Imbolg, letting the new year sleep in the snow and be born with the lambs in spring. You may choose differently, as many do, letting Samhain mark the beginning of the season of the dead, the Dark Mother, the time when what is over and without energy falls away as we wait for the sun to be reborn.

Questions to Ponder
Consider the following as you shuffle your deck. What is our relationship to our ancestors? It may be problematic or untenable, and we may have turned away from our lineages and reached out instead to the ancestors of the Indigenous people on whose land we live. There will come a time when we all need to do the work necessary on our own lineages, no matter how (or perhaps especially because of how) painful or ugly it may be. What is the work we need to do to strengthen ourselves before engaging with our lineages? What are we not willing to look at? Where can we go for help in reaching out to our ancestors in a healthy and safe way?

Southern Hemisphere
How do you connect with the land you live on and its people? How do you relate to your beloved (and not-so-beloved) dead? It may not be as easy to speak to them if it's sunny and warm and bright where you are, but just because the vibe is different doesn't mean the energy is—a thin veil is a thin veil, right? How would you want to celebrate the joy of Bealtaine with loved ones who are gone, if they could be there with you? Is there a way to honor them now in your celebrations, through sharing their stories, pictures, memories, or songs?

Spread
After shuffling, draw seven cards and lay them out according to the following diagram.

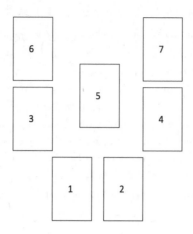

Positions

1. ***What does my relationship to my ancestors look like right now?*** This is one of those "begin where you are" questions. What does the landscape look like? Do you have any ancestral connection at all? Sometimes if a person is adopted or has a parent who is adopted, the whole concept of ancestral connection can feel moot. It's not, though. Here is an opportunity to begin at the beginning, whether you have no connections or multiple generations of wisdom at hand.

2. ***How can I honor my dead at this time?*** The answer will be different for everybody, and it may not be quite what you think. It will likely vary from one year to the next. Maybe your ancestors want something from you now that they've never asked for before. Maybe you're at a time in your life when you're noticing things more, feeling things more. What do they want you to do right now?

3. ***What work do I need to do to strengthen myself and my lineages?*** Maybe you can start work on your family tree. There are a variety of resources online to begin building

from, and if that's not your style, there are old-school methods like calling records offices, writing letters, and maybe even talking to your elders (there's a thought). This position might also bring up psychological or emotional issues that need to be dealt with; be honest with yourself about whether or not you could use some help.

4. *What about my ancestry do I not want to look at?* If we have no history or tradition around noticing or talking about our family shadows, we need to start one, and now is as good a time as any. It's important to talk about our ancestral issues as a doorway into healing, and also to practice seeing our dead as people, however flawed they may have been. This may be a difficult question, so take whatever time you need with it.[6]

5. *What do I need to let go of, to release into the grave of the old year?* Are you holding on to anything that can be released? Are you living out any lineage drama that you don't have to? Because that baggage can absolutely go.

6. *What steps can I take in the world to begin to remedy any damage my people may have done while they were alive?* Here we have the homework position of the Samhain spread. Our ancestors can help us with messages, warnings, wisdom, etc., and we can help them by working to undo or fix issues they created, or added to, or weren't able to fix themselves. We might not be able to fix them ourselves either—some issues took lifetimes to create, so

6 It's very important to note here that it is absolutely not necessary to approach abusive, threatening, or dangerous ancestors to do this spread or any ancestor work. By all means, bypass those ones if they exist in your lineages and reach back to your healed and whole ones (we all have them), even if you don't know their names, and even if you have to go back a thousand years. Don't engage with the abusive ones at all; go over their heads (so to speak) and reach farther back in time, asking instead for assistance from "the healed, whole, mighty, beloved dead of my lineages" as a collective entity.

they may take lifetimes to re-create. But we can make a
start out in the real world, and that's the important thing.

7. *What message do my ancestors have for me this*
   Samhain?

Sample Reading

The spread of cards here balances Major and Minor Arcana
cards, and there is also a balance of light and shadow—the dark
elements and colors play up against the bright ones, and the mix
of Fire and Water imagery suggests that this will be a reading
of the heart more than of the mind or body. Almost everything
we see here leans toward individual expression and experience,
so it makes sense to proceed with the reading from that point of
view—that is, we might learn more about the self in relationship
to the sacred other than we would about the self in connection
with community or the hive. The ancestors we're hoping to
reach through this spread are speaking to us about our heart and
passions rather than our position and actions in the wider world,
so the whole reading has the comfortable, cozy vibe of having tea
and a chat in the kitchen with a member of your Other-Side Team
as you work out your issues together.

1. *What does my relationship to my ancestors look like*
   right now? The Ace of Pentacles. The Aces in the Tarot
   represent beginnings, but looks can be deceiving, so don't
   look at the card and think, "I'm not a beginner!" This Ace
   is all about putting ideas *into practice*. That's the key here.

2. *How can I honor my dead at this time?* The Moon card
   is all kinds of complicated, as is our relationship with the
   dead for so many of us. The moon doesn't emit any light
   of its own; it reflects the light of the sun. This is true
   for our ancestors as well—they don't exist in this realm
   anymore, but they are reflected in us, by us, by our actions
   and our lives in the world around us. We honor them by

being honorable. We can and should be our truest selves, which are both wild and civilized, and we can speak from the depths of the unknown within us in whatever language comes naturally from that place.

3. *What work do I need to do to strengthen myself and my lineages?* The 8 of Swords is a card of worry, mistakes, worry about mistakes, and unfounded fear about worry and/or mistakes. If things feel complicated or overwhelming, start slow. Take things one little step at a time, and trust your gut and your common sense. That might be something your ancestors got good at during their lives, and it might be something they can help you with.

4. *What about my ancestry do I not want to look at?* The High Priestess is a card of great intuition, wisdom, and inner knowing—it's the more private, intuition-driven counterpart to the Hierophant, who relies more on the lore and scriptures and is much less inclined to wing it when working with the divine than the High Priestess, who always trusts her intuition. Maybe your ancestors were good at this kind of thing; maybe they can help you recover this belief in yourself.

5. *What do I need to let go of, to release into the grave of the old year?* The 2 of Wands is a card of control, power, and management. Our ancestors are telling us that we need to let go of the illusion of control, or of thinking that we need to control everything, because we don't. We can't. Let the grave take your need to control everything.

6. *What steps can I take in the world to begin to remedy any damage my people may have done while they were alive?* The Devil card is scary, it's true, and his backstory is epically awful; but here he can be incredibly helpful. The

Devil has elements of the Trickster, and the Trickster isn't inherently bad. Tricksters are chaotic free thinkers and move in unexpected ways to shake up the status quo. We are being called to speak truth to power.

7. *What message do my ancestors have for me this Samhain?* The Chariot is a card of powerful forward movement and energy, a crystal-clear cosmic "YES" that encourages us to go for it. Whatever it is, go for it. Take a chance, call on your ancestors for support, and then leap! The power and energy of Samhain is a perfect time to gather up our plans, toss the luggage into the trunk, slap some lipstick on, and get out on the road!

November

THE FULL MOON

There's an unofficial tradition here in the States in which we moan about the first holiday television commercial of the season, which usually appears in early November. There's even a cartoon floating around that shows a grumpy turkey in a pilgrim's hat kicking Santa Claus out of the stores until after the turkey has had his turn. Whatever humor is inherent in poultry hollering angrily at a human figure, it's a sign of how commercialized this time of year has become and how performative everything can be, and that's not especially funny. Have we lost the meaning of Thanksgiving celebrations by focusing too much on trying to make it perfect? To be honest with you, Thanksgiving is my least-favorite holiday, if for no other reason than the stress of trying to help pull it all together (although the colonial roots of the holiday are certainly problematic and ugly and don't stand up to close scrutiny). It isn't that I don't love my families of blood and the heart; I do, very dearly. But I don't love the pressure I feel to create something—a vibe that's literally over in twenty minutes because that's how long it takes folks to eat—and I definitely don't love washing up afterwards. But I do love spending time with family, sharing stories, laughing, talking, and just being together. That makes it worth all the work.

This is the time when, even though it seems like everything is speeding up, we can do our best to slow down. While some holiday traditions are wonderful, are we stressing ourselves out for no reason? Have we forgotten that no matter what we're told, from whatever source, the full moon in November is a time when we can stop the wild ride and just be grateful for where we are and who we're with, what we've learned and where we've come from? Whether or not you celebrate some form of Thanksgiving holiday in November, building the time into your schedule to stop, look around, and breathe is a gift and a blessing worth giving yourself.

The Full Moon—Southern Hemisphere

How do you express gratitude in your life? What are your expectations around it? For better or worse, Thanksgiving is an American and Canadian thing, but the ideas behind it work everywhere. How can we share more and reach out to each other in friendship and compassion? How can we celebrate and even enjoy our differences? What would a Thanksgiving dinner look like at your place? If the theme was "gratitude," how would you express it?

THE DARK MOON

There's a drama inherent in November that you'd think I'd love as an emotional Pisces child. There's that fierce Scorpio energy that dares you to follow along and then reaches out for you when you turn away. November is the month of feasting and family, both of which have their light, beautiful side and their dark, terrible side. November is also a month of bad memories for the US: a few years before I was born, John F. Kennedy was assassinated in November; fifteen years later, George Moscone and Harvey Milk were gunned down in their offices in San Francisco in November; and the dreadful Peoples Temple massacre at Jonestown, Guyana, happened in November. These last events loomed large in my life, growing up near San Francisco as I did. My congressional representative for many years was the Honorable Jackie Speier, who was shot five times by members of the Peoples Temple on the day of the massacre and went on to thrive in community service, both locally and nationally. Whenever I see her on TV or hear her speak, I think with a sense of hometown pride of what she overcame on that awful November day. But the Jonestown massacre still haunts me, because it's the very worst that can happen when a community devours itself out of fear, isolation, and hatred of anything other. At this time of year, during the dark moon of November, we can take time to look into the shadows to see how we retreat from the other, how we run away from community or turn inward in an unhealthy way, so that we can practice banishing our nightmares in ways that serve us without doing damage to those who care about us.

The Dark Moon—Southern Hemisphere
How do you balance alone time with community time? Everyone is different, of course—we're all a mix of introverts and extroverts and introverted extroverts and extroverted introverts—but we are a social species in the main, and we need each other to survive. How do you find yourself taking adequate alone time amidst community engagements, of which there tend to be many at this time of year? Or do you avoid being alone entirely? Do you chase away the shadows with constant action, not allowing yourself a moment's introspection? How can you use this time to explore your connection to community as it is in the moment?

NOVEMBER FULL MOON
Keywords
Gratitude, family, connection, peace

Questions to Ponder
Consider the following as you shuffle your deck. This is usually the time of year in the United States when we focus on gratitude and counting our blessings; what does that mean for us? Have we ever tried literally counting the things we're grateful for? It's an interesting experience that can be useful as a way out of Anxiety Mind when things are challenging or painful. But it might bring a new awareness to elements of life to be grateful for. My Dad used to joke about a kid who was digging through a huge pile

of poop, and when asked why, he said, "There's gotta be a pony in here somewhere!" It's a funny reminder to me to approach all situations with a sense of humor if I can, but also to try to find the pony in the pile of poop. Where's our pony? Are we focusing more on the pile that we all have to dig through at times, or on finding the pony in there somewhere? As the days get shorter and the darkness grows all around us, where can we find the light? Where can we be a light for others?

Spread

After shuffling, draw four cards and lay them out according to the following diagram.

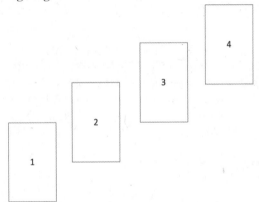

Positions

1. *Where in my life do I need to stop?* Where does the sacred pause need to happen? We might wish that we could take a break from everything and run off to join the circus (whatever that might look like for you) and never come back, but that's not a viable option for most of us. So where can we stop the madness in a way that works in our lives? Where can we make changes that are effective and realistic, and that give us the break we probably need?

2. *What tools can I use to disconnect from the frantic year-end energy all around me?* It's easy enough to say, "Turn off the phone!" But that's not an option for everybody, and often the phone isn't the problem. The apps aren't the problem. If we can discover what we're chasing or what we're trying so frantically to keep up with, then we can figure out what needs to go on time-out for a while—and it might not be the phone.

3. *What do I have to be grateful for that I'm not seeing clearly?* Where are our blind spots? They're blind spots for a reason—maybe something is a blessing in disguise? Even in bad times, even amidst darkness or fear, there are still stars to wish on. Where in our lives are these hidden stars, and how can we find them?

4. *How can I show more gratitude in my life in a real way?* Consider this the homework portion of the spread. How can we take what we've learned and actually do something with it that helps us and also helps others? Gratitude is a gift best shared, right?

Sample Reading

These cards give us a lot to work with. There's movement in each card, although it's more implied than expressed in some places. None of the figures are looking directly at us except the Queen of Wands (and the Fool's dog); we can't see if the figure walking away from us in the 8 of Cups has their eyes open or not, but either way there's a sense of moving forward from whatever went before—sort of pausing and then stepping forward into the unknown in a way that reflects the dance the Fool does. And speaking of the Fool, we've got one Major Arcana card and two court cards in this spread, so we may see more information about individuals or groups of people rather than life activities. Everybody at least seems open, so that's a start!

1. ***Where in my life do I need to stop?*** The 8 of Cups is a card of obvious movement. So yes, the Tarot is telling us, we need to stop moving right now. We need to let life catch up.

2. ***What tools can I use to disconnect from the frantic year-end energy all around me?*** The Fool tells us it's time to break some rules, set aside old boundaries, get rid of old baggage. Let go, jump, and see where you land! Create new ways that work for you, and listen to your body to see what's comfortable and what feels right.

3. ***What do I have to be grateful for that I'm not seeing clearly?*** The Page of Cups shows us that we're not paying enough attention to our intuition, the part of ourselves that plumbs the depths of the unconscious mind and the mysteries of the heart. This is our voice, our own language, and we need to start listening.

4. *How can I show more gratitude in my life in a real way?* The Queen of Wands is the "manspreading" queen, She Who Takes Up Room, and there is nothing about her that hides. In the Rider-Waite-Smith Tarot deck, she is the only queen who faces the reader directly. Here in the Divine Deco Tarot, she's also dancing and channeling her fire. She is in the world, full of fire and life. Her presence here tells us to make our gratitude known and to not be shy about it.

NOVEMBER DARK MOON

Keywords
Solitude, rejection, illness, worry

Questions to Ponder
Consider the following as you shuffle your deck. Where do we run when we're afraid? What is our distraction (or addiction) of choice, our numbing-out agent that helps us face (or ignore) the darkness? What excuse do we use to shut others out, drown them out, and reject their attempts to draw us in? There's nothing wrong with alone time, of course, but there's a difference between healthy alone time and cutting oneself off from community entirely. We all need community, even as individuals; we all need connection to grow and thrive, no matter how much we've bought into the idea of "rugged individualism" on a national level in the US. So how do we feed the "cowboy" beast? What do we sacrifice to that false god that would have us believe that individualism is both possible and a desirable thing? How can we make the idea and the practice of engaging with community more palatable to us, especially if we're introverted or otherwise need or prefer time alone?

Spread

After shuffling, draw five cards and lay them out according to the following diagram.

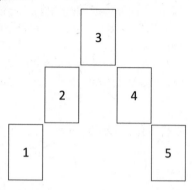

Positions

1. *What part of me am I sacrificing by trying to go it alone right now?* We may think that there's no sacrifice involved, or that the sacrifice is worth it because other people just suck sometimes. However, we need to know what we're doing to ourselves in the cold light of day, so that we can choose more freely in case we've gotten ourselves into a pickle that we aren't even aware of. What is being cut off as we cut ourselves off? We know what we gain by separating ourselves from community (peace and quiet, for one thing), but what are we *losing* by separating ourselves from community?

2. *What am I not seeing by shutting myself off from others?* The unseen drawbacks of isolation can do some serious damage before we even know they exist. What will be the unintentional consequences of isolation at this time?

3. *How can I make being in community more palatable and workable for me?* When we're surrounded by people

(or even in a group of only two or three others), what do we need in the moment to help us feel more present, more grounded, and less overwhelmed? How can we turn being in community from tedium—or even danger—into something empowering and celebratory? We do this not so that we can make ourselves into something we're not, but rather to help us enjoy the human connection that's our birthright.

4. *What does my "Solo Self," the small voice that represents me at my core and speaks when everything else is quiet, want to tell me in this moment?*

5. *What does my "People Self," the face I wear around others and the part of me that connects to my community, want to tell me in this moment?*

Sample Reading

This is another spread that shows us mostly solitary figures having their own processes and feeling some kind of way about it, moving through energy and experience by the power of their own giddy-up. You may notice that some of the figures in these cards present as male, through which we can apply a layer of action-oriented direction to the reading; perhaps this is one of the readings from which we can expect to walk away with homework or action items. There is one Major Arcana card and one King, indicating action from a place of awareness and great confidence; but, interestingly, only the charioteer faces us directly. We see the figure in the 2 of Wands from behind, so can hardly see his face, and while we face the figure in the 7 of Wands almost directly, her focus is on the wands coming up from below her. And of course the thief in the 7 of Swords isn't even watching where he's going; all his focus is on the action behind him, maybe to make sure he isn't being chased. Even the King of Cups is looking away, strangely insecure perhaps, as if he's afraid we'll see his bad side if we see him straight on. There's a handsome American television news anchor I've seen who does the same thing, turning his head to the left while looking into the camera before him. I've often wondered why he does that as he delivers the evening news, and I wonder the same about this King. Handsome and emotional, masterful and in command of his element, he may still be haunted by skepticism and self-doubt when working through the questions meant to uncover the mysteries of the shadow self.

1. *What part of me am I sacrificing by trying to go it alone right now?* The 2 of Wands is all about confidence and command, about knowing and believing in one's own power and will to accomplish great things. By not connecting with others in a way that's healthy for us right now, we're sacrificing leadership possibilities and connections with colleagues we maybe haven't met yet, and we're also sacrificing balance.

2. *What am I not seeing by shutting myself off from others?* The Chariot card shows us what we're not seeing when we shut ourselves off from others, and if it wasn't clear that working well with others creates opportunities for success, it should be clear now. We are not seeing how to achieve wins by working with others. The Chariot in this position assures us that the rewards are great if we collaborate.

3. *How can I make being in community more palatable and workable for me?* The King of Cups, the master of the emotional and mysterious realm of the heart, is both artistic and mindful of how his art is used (and paid for!) in the world. He can teach us a lot about being our complete selves while also not giving too much away.

4. *What does my "Solo Self," the small voice that represents me at my core and speaks when everything else is quiet, want to tell me in this moment?* The 7 of

Wands, another card of victory—but this time there's an element of fighting for the prize and holding on to it. The "Solo Self" card is telling us, "You've got this!" and that we have both the right and the responsibility to ourselves to acknowledge it.

5. *What does my "People Self," the face I wear around others and the part of me that connects to my community, want to tell me in this moment?* The 7 of Swords is, among other things, the card of thievery and hidden dangers. As we step out into the world of other people, we will invariably run into those who suck. It's just the way of things. How we respond to these thefts is up to us, though; we are not entirely without agency to recognize these people and disengage before they can create damage—or to establish strong boundaries if circumstances require us to remain in contact with them.

December

THE FULL MOON

*A*s we look to close out the calendar year, December's full moon gives us a chance to stop, reflect, and let the joy of the season wash over us. It's true that in the midst of a whirl of holiday activity, it might be a challenge to find time to reflect on whether or not our socks match, let alone to do the inner work called for by this full moon. But it's worth the attempt to connect with our inner hermit for a little while and see what comes up. The weather at this time of year will of course depend on where you live and how climate change is affecting your area, but it's probably safe to say that in most places in the Northern Hemisphere, December's full moon lives up to its sometime-nickname the "Cold Moon." As winter and increasing darkness descend upon the northern world, we move indoors to avoid wind, snow, and rain, and shorter days lend themselves to longer, quieter nights with plenty of time to think. As the holidays approach and year-end celebrations get going, we are led to review the ending year and ask ourselves all the questions that the fussy light of day chases off with her endless to-do lists and errands, her work schedules and homeschooling, her child or elder care. The full moon of December hangs quiet and bright, inviting us to take the time to go within and light our own way through the darkness to see what gifts might be found there and brought back, for our own benefit and for the benefit of those around us.

The Full Moon—Southern Hemisphere

In societies that recognize the winter holidays, the issues will be the same: the time crunch and schedule mishaps, the gift giving and parties, the challenges that come up at the end of the calendar year (like loneliness, fatigue, and stress) will all be the same—only the weather will be different. And that has its own challenges, I'm sure! But it's also a good time to reflect on how the holiday themes and traditions play out in every culture, what's different, what's better about the holidays where you live than on the other side of the world, and what keeps you connected to your people. This is also the time of the turning of the year, so doing some kind of year-end round-up review is certainly worthwhile during this December full moon.

THE DARK MOON

It's a fair bet that we all walk a sometimes-precarious line between what we want to do and what we have to do. Sometimes we have more of an opportunity to do what we want, but life in general tends to command that we do what we have to do to get by. Or perhaps it's not that grim. Maybe it's not all fated to be struggle and obligation and duty from birth to death. Maybe we flow in a constantly churning continuum between ups and downs, and no one would blame us for wanting the ups to go on forever and the downs to be much shallower and shorter than they usually end up being. During December, when the social media flood is set to "joy tsunami" whether it's our reality or not, the lows can get dark and long. We can develop an insidious perception that everyone else has it all figured out and is enjoying the perfect holiday with the perfect family, while our reality is poverty, family drama, and weight gain. So where is the truth? Where's the line between what's real and what's a projection of our own wounded psyche? Can we reset our internal "preferences" so that the pervasive lies about what should be take their proper place? Can we remove the blinders that keep us from seeing and understanding our experiences as they actually are, rather than as we wish they were? What comprises our blinders, and do we even know we have them on? What are our excuses? These are the reasons we give as to why we can't do things or have what we want or live the lives we wish we could.

I remember taking a self-actualization workshop in the 1990s. During a session where we learned about our blinders and the lenses that affect our perceptions, every time someone would say, "I want to do this thing, but I can't because of . . ." whatever the reason was, the workshop leader would respond by saying, "But if you could, what would it look like?" And after this happened a few times to different people in the workshop, we all began to get the idea that we wouldn't be able to use the "but I can't because" excuse anymore. We would all be forced to face the reasons for our failure or rejection, and the fact that we created those reasons ourselves. The goalposts somehow move when we get close to our goals, but are we the ones who are moving them? Or at the very least, do we make it easy to miss out on what we want by turning away from it when it appears, for reasons related to annoying but unavoidable obligations? What is a real obstacle to be surmounted, and what is us inventing an alien invasion to get out of trying?

The Dark Moon—Southern Hemisphere

Do you find yourself moving your own goalposts so that you don't have to finish something and be judged harshly by others, or fail, or—worse—succeed and have to deal with the changes that result? Where do you withdraw from the world and give everybody the finger so that they'll leave you alone, even if what you need most is their assistance? Is the energy around you now pulling inward so hard that nobody could get near you if they tried? Where's the balance for you between obligation to yourself and obligation to others, and how can you create healthier boundaries around it?

DECEMBER FULL MOON

Keywords
Pause, rest, gifts, endings

Questions to Ponder
Consider the following as you shuffle your deck. How will we answer for our time this past year? What didn't work, and what did? What changes did we have to make, and why? Do we have time to take a general pause right now, or is everything the chaotic whirl that tends to be the norm in December? How will we mark the passing of the year? Will we take special note of the losses, the wins, or both? Where do we land on the gift-giving spectrum? Some folks love giving everyone a present for the holidays, and other folks direct their gift giving only to the children in their lives. I know a man who refuses to give gifts at the holidays, and while I try not to judge him for it, he's judging me for participating in what he perceives as the consumerist layers of purchased holiday cheer, and I'm sure he's not the only one. And it's fine, truly: he can judge me until the cows come home—I'm an avowed present giver. But at the core of the tradition of gift giving at this time of year, which has recently become more about "getting That Thing" than it ever was before, there's a reciprocity; it's important to remember where the tradition came from and why we give each other things. We need each other. We are connected by obligations and commitments, by relationships that are strengthened by gift exchange. The mistake we make is in thinking that the gifts must be purchased or made, when in fact they can be a beloved book from our bookshelf, or an article of clothing or a purse or a piece of jewelry from our closet—something to help the recipient remember us and to tell them that we remember and love them.

Spread

After shuffling, draw six cards and lay them out according to the following diagram.

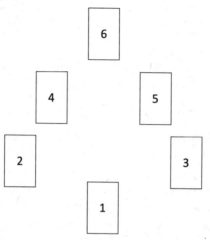

Positions

1. *How can I adjust my schedule of obligations to make room for some quiet contemplation?* I imagine this is the question most of us ask at least once during every holiday season: Where can I find some "me" time? What do I need to cut out? As much as connections and relationships are important, the most important connection and relationship we'll have is with ourselves. So how can we shift some priorities around to make time to just sit and be quiet for a little while?

2. *In what area of my life have the lights gone out and need to be relit?* The days tend to be hard right now—maybe they always were, but things seem to be more intense at this time of year, and we can lose our light pretty easily. I'm not one who believes that once a person's light goes out it's out forever, though. I believe in the eternal power

of relighting that flame the minute you notice it's out, but noticing it can be a challenge, especially if we're distracted. So where do we need to relight our passion for life? And is there a window somewhere that we need to close so a draft doesn't blow in? Because let's close that window, for sure.

3. *What do I need to know about the coming year?* Let's ask the Tarot for a hint. Come on, you know you want to.

4. *What is my gift-giving "profile" and how can I learn from it?* Sometimes this can be a blind spot. Are we someone who gives and says they want nothing in return but secretly does want something? Are we honest with ourselves and others about our expectations? Unmet expectations destroy a lot of goodwill, so it's important to keep them in check.

5. *What gift does Spirit have for me now that I'm not seeing?* Sometimes the best presents are the ones we've had all along and just never noticed. There are times when I'd love the answer to a question like this to be "here are jewels and books and free time," but I'm pretty sure Spirit doesn't shop. Looking beyond the material, what gifts have we been given that we're not seeing because we're expecting something else, or because we have some work to do in learning to believe in ourselves?

6. *How can I share the gift of myself with others in the coming year?* Sometimes the best part of presents is sharing them. How can we share what we receive with others so that they can receive it, too?

Sample Reading

There are no Major Arcana cards in this spread and only one court card (the King of Wands), and there are no Swords (Air) cards at all, so it's probably safe to assume that this reading is going to be fairly low to the ground and not too worried about our mental efforts. There are two Aces, representing sources and origins, and everybody represented here looks to be young and in varying states of confusion or annoyance, which seems pretty *de rigueur* for December. But we have an opportunity to see how we see ourselves and how we function when we're not looking, and it looks like we're being brought gifts by Spirit, even if we don't notice them right away.

1. *How can I adjust my schedule of obligations to make room for some quiet contemplation?* The 4 of Cups. Perhaps finding that quiet time isn't quite as difficult as we think it is. Maybe it's actually *right there* for us, and all we have to do is get our minds off ourselves and consider the world around us, and we'll find it.

2. *In what area of my life have the lights gone out and need to be relit?* The Ace of Wands is the card of sacred spark, the initial fire of passion and joy, so dreaming big is definitely required here. If money wasn't an issue (or time, or anything else), what would you do? What would your passion be? Think big!

3. *What do I need to know about the coming year?* The Ace of Cups tells us that the coming year will be a heart-people year, maybe even a falling-in-love year, which is a sweet and lovely thought. If it's not about finding romance for you, it's about discovering and learning to love yourself first, about putting your own mask on first and not sacrificing your own need to breathe while trying to save others.

4. *What is my gift-giving "profile" and how can I learn from it?* The 2 of Pentacles is a card in motion, a dancer through life, juggling the new and the strange together with whatever comes in as each new day dawns. It's still possible to laugh and respond creatively even in challenging times. Sharing happiness is a worthy gift, and it's free.

5. *What gift does Spirit have for me now that I'm not seeing?* The 5 of Wands, a card of creative struggle and confusion, which is the gift: whatever creative struggle is happening is meaningful because we're working something out, learning how to do The Thing without being in danger of real consequences if we fail. Let yourself be in the struggle and don't be afraid of making mistakes.

6. *How can I share the gift of myself with others in the coming year?* The King of Wands has figured out what needs to be done and how to do it; he knows how

to develop his passion, from the spark of an idea in the Ace of Wands, through the awkward brawl phase of the 5 of Wands, into something graceful and elegant that will serve others in whatever way it needs to once it has manifested in the material world.

DECEMBER DARK MOON

Keywords
Excess, denial, compression

Questions to Ponder
Consider the following as you shuffle your deck. Where is the line between what's real and what's imagined? Are things really as bad (or as good, or as whatever) as we think they are, or are we making everything harder by injecting it with fear? What truth are we not seeing, and what do we need to do to start seeing what's real? Is there a reason why we're not seeing the truth around us? Because there very well might be, and it may be a legitimate need to stay in the dark about something right now. Or are we just scared and not ready to take responsibility for fixing whatever needs fixing? How can we move past our fear and empower ourselves to take the actions we need to take to clarify what's really going on?

Spread
After shuffling, draw five cards and lay them out according to the following diagram.

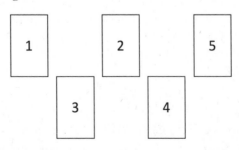

Positions

1. *Show me what I want to do.* This might not be quite the slam dunk you think it is, and that's part of what's so tricky about questions like this. We think we want one thing, or the conscious part of ourselves wants one thing, but our unconscious self might not be in alignment with it, and it's good to know that. We might want to go to medical school, but our unconscious self might want to be off in Morocco learning to bake khobz, so getting into better alignment with what the unconscious self has going on is a good start.

2. *Show me what I have to do.* If med school is a requirement, then let's see it. Let's quantify what must be done because there's nothing else for it. And sometimes it's more useful to have this shown to us in a visual, symbolic manner, so that we can both perceive it and start thinking about it in different, more creative ways. Or if we only *think* med school is what's most needful right now but there's really something much more important going on, then we need to know that, too.

3. *What is the line between what I want to do and what I have to do, and is it real or imagined?* What are my goalposts? Am I moving them around on myself when I'm not looking? What is my perception of reality, and what's actual reality? What excuses am I telling myself for not making changes in my life?

4. *Why am I making excuses for not pursuing what I want?* What am I getting out of staying put and not taking the necessary risks? There's always an upside, a reason for staying in the dark, and finding out what it is is useful for either moving past it or at least being more honest with ourselves about the roots of our motivations.

203

5. *What's one step I can take to start seeing everything more clearly?* Action items! Let's take away an action item that will help us understand more clearly where we are and how to begin making changes.

Sample Reading

The cards presented in this spread seem to be talking about everyday events and tasks, with no Major Arcana cards, and only the Knight of Swords to bring high-speed movement and processing. There's movement in each of the cards, but it takes the Knight in the last card to really put the pedal to the metal. Everybody here is doing something, going somewhere—even the figure in the Ace of Wands card looks like it's about to summon some powerful energy and create something great and magical. But is it where we want to go, where we need to go, or just circular movement to keep us alive, like land sharks afraid to stop moving? It's also interesting to note that there are two 10s in this spread. The 10s indicate completion of a cycle or taking some form of action or belief to its conclusion. Since the 10s here are in the realm of Cups (Water) and Wands (Fire), any solution we take away from them will likely be from other realms, and perhaps our emotions are too strong to see it without help.

1. *Show me what I want to do.* The 10 of Cups. This card is about having everything your heart desires to be happy. While what it takes to be happy will be different for everyone, the desire to be rooted in family and community is important to all of us. So we need to keep that awareness front and center as we explore where we are and what we have to do. This card shows us that what we desire is to be happy no matter what we're doing, so finding a way to make that happen is the work.

2. *Show me what I have to do.* The 7 of Swords is a card of thieving and trickery, so unless we have to steal to

get by, there's an indication here that what we think we have to do is not really what we have to do. We're kidding ourselves or lying to ourselves about something, and somebody is definitely taking advantage of it.

3. *What is the line between what I want to do and what I have to do, and is it real or imagined?* The Ace of Wands carries with it the divine spark to create anything. This means that the line between what we want to do and what we have to do is one that we create ourselves. Look carefully at your schedule and see where there might be padding or distractions that can be cut. What can be let go of? And as for whether the line between our responsibilities and our desires is real or imagined, the suit of Wands exists within us. It is the fire that drives us to create what we want or need in our lives. So while it might not be as real in the manifest world as the Ace of Pentacles, for example, it's still real enough to us to make it worth paying attention to.

4. *Why am I making excuses for not pursuing what I want?* The 10 of Wands is a card of burdens and blindness, of struggling through to get where we need to go because there's nothing else to be done. It's a card of overwhelm and exhaustion, of doing too much all at the same time. We can't even see the path in front of us for all the burdens we're carrying.

5. *What's one step I can take to start seeing everything more clearly?* The Knight of Swords is the one Knight in the Tarot who moves like lightning. The moment they think of something somewhere, they're there. The ideas, the thoughts, the words need to flow. We need to start speaking into existence what we want and what we need—to be clear and forceful about it and let no one stand in our way.

KNIGHT OF SWORDS

ACE OF WANDS

Winter Solstice

Keywords

Balance, tipping point, silence, seeing through the darkness

*T*t may seem strange or counterintuitive to think of the Winter Solstice as a time of silence. The hullaballoo at this time of year is considerable, and just hearing oneself think in the middle of it, let alone making time to quiet the outer and inner noise in order to be able to tune into the movement of the cosmos, is a huge accomplishment. Yet that tuning in is exactly what the Winter Solstice is perfect for: practicing that arabesque of stillness required to hold steady and listen to the Great Wheel turn, before leaping once more into the dance of the living as the Wheel moves us toward the return of the light. This solstice is often called "Yule" and is historically the time for giving and receiving gifts, sharing light and warmth amidst a frozen landscape, and celebrating community. It's also a time for retreat, for contemplation and planning, and, perhaps above all, for rest. "What is this 'rest' sorcery you speak of?" you may ask, because many segments of Western culture tend to demonize the very concept of resting, let alone the enactment of it. There are multiple layers of value in setting aside time to rest at various points in the year, and the solstices are perfect times to do so because they require stillness, a pause to take a breath prior to moving into whatever comes next.

The Winter Solstice is the moment when the sun is reborn and the light returns to the Northern Hemisphere. It is the shortest day of the year and the longest night, making it a perfect time for introspection, quiet, rest, and silence. When we think about the return of the sun and the light, it's not just the astronomical effects we're considering. It's a reminder that things are always changing, that the sun gods who sacrifice themselves for their people are reborn every year, and that change brings life.

Questions to Ponder

Consider the following as you shuffle your deck. What does this moment of pause and reflection mean to us? Is this something that's a struggle to make time for? What value is there in going quiet for a while? What is Spirit trying to tell us that we will only be able to hear if we stop and go silent to listen? How can this moment of darkness shine light on the unseen and unknown questions in our lives? What stories do we have about moving from dark to light, about movement and pause, about stopping and letting it all wash over us? What stories do we have about the voice or voices that will speak if we go silent, about what we'll hear that maybe we are afraid to hear? What needs to be left behind in the dark, to be buried and mourned so that forward movement can happen as the sun and life return?

Southern Hemisphere

If it's useful for you, please feel free to switch the spreads and read the Summer Solstice one in December and the Winter Solstice one in June.

Balance, stillness, and the concept of a passage through a liminal space are up and big right now in both hemispheres, although what will happen once the tipping point is passed will of course be different. But the questions can be considered just the same, no matter where on earth we are. We have the opportunity to take the time during the December solstice to let ourselves pause and embrace a moment of stillness, no matter how loud and busy things may be around us.

Spread

After shuffling, draw seven cards and lay them out according to the following diagram.

Positions

1. *What value is there in going quiet for a while that I'm not seeing?* Sometimes it helps to know what can be gained from an action before acting, especially if we aren't predisposed to find value in that action in the first place. Sometimes we need convincing. So let's ask what we get out of periods of stillness that we're not seeing. We can listen to the health experts talk about meditation until we're blue in the face, but unless we understand on a root level how we benefit from a mindfulness practice, we're never going to make time to do it. What's in our blind spot here?

2. *What is most important for me to know right now, in this moment of stillness?* What do we need to remember during this sacred pause? What is the image, memory, thought, or metaphor that we can hang on to? What do

we need to be reminded of to help us make the most of this time?

3. *What truth is Spirit trying to tell me that I'm not hearing?* No matter what the reason, sometimes it's just hard to hear things. Whether we're not ready or unwilling or whatever, we all need help every now and again to hear what's most important. The truth can be entirely different than what we think it is, and we need a reality recalibration to bring us back into alignment with what we need to be doing.

4. *What should I bury and leave behind in darkness? What died when I wasn't looking?* It's never a good idea to drag your dead around. It's unsanitary and unhelpful, and it announces you to friend and foe alike whether you want it to or not. Are you carrying your dead without even knowing you're doing it? Time to identify what needs to be released and then release it.

5. *What is my North Star right now, my guiding principle?* What can you hang on to when all else is darkness, fear, and loss? You might be surprised to learn that you have more strength than you think you do; you just need to know where to look.

6. *How can I shine my light brighter for my own benefit and that of others?* Once the light begins to grow, how can you share it? Maybe others are farther back in the darkness than you are; how can you reach for them and send them hope that they, too, can make it into the light?

7. *What is waiting to be born with the sun in my life?* What will the new season of light and life bring, and how can I help manifest it?

Sample Reading

We have all suits represented in this draw, as well as cards from both Major and Minor Arcana. We have royalty and commoners here, and humans and non-humans too. While the Moon card represents the reflected light of nighttime, the figures in most of the other cards seem to be in the full light of day. Here, we have clarity, vision, and open possibilities. While there is confusion and sadness in the 3 of Swords, everything else seems to bear witness to victory—hard-fought, hard-won victory. As we pause at this great tipping point in the year and look at the cards, we see a balance of warm and cool colors, of clarity and mystery, and of familiar tropes and startling symbolism that together need some parsing out.

1. *What value is there in going quiet for a while that I'm not seeing?* The 3 of Swords. With the exception of the 10 of Swords, I find the 3 of Swords to be the most high-drama card in the Rider-Waite-Smith Tarot because of its powerful symbolism of the heart's complete overthrow by the mind. There is great sorrow we are not seeing, and we need to see it in order to move on. We need to process grief in order to feel joy.

2. *What is most important for me to know right now, in this moment of stillness?* The Page of Pentacles is warm and kind and reminds us that there are always things we can do to help ourselves and others. We can use our imagination and remember that we're not without agency. The important thing is to try, to have faith in our vision, to look at a blank space or fallow field or empty building or vacant lot and see what it could be, and then make the plan that gets us there.

3. *What truth is Spirit trying to tell me that I'm not hearing?* The Queen of Swords delivers the message of the Page of Pentacles in a strange sort of role reversal

that's pretty cool, actually. The pages are the messengers of the Tarot, but if their messages can't get through, here comes the Queen of Swords to cut through the nonsense. The Queen here is telling us to pay attention, to focus. Stop messing around with polite words and kind but confusing metaphors. Speak up. Speak your truth and let your words carry the weight they're meant to.

4. *What should I bury and leave behind in darkness?* The Knight of Cups is the commander-in-chief of speaking around the point in meandering, dainty circles. He's a dreamer who is not into engaging in painful feelings, so he'll wander for hours trying to find a way around a difficult crossing, rather than just cowgirling up, wading across, and getting through it—which is exactly what needs to happen. This shilly-shallying way of communicating our heart's truest desires has got to go. Listen to the Queen above: speak out, speak up, be honest, and let your words carry their weight.

5. *What is my North Star right now, my guiding principle?* The Queen of Wands is the ruler of both passions and boundaries, allowing both to grow while keeping both in check. She is about command, about the passion that drives clear vision forward and moves plans from incubation to generative work. Here she is our North Star, that voice within us telling us with great certainty that it's time to get to work.

6. *How can I shine my light brighter for my own benefit and that of others?* The 6 of Wands. The message here is to accept the accolades of victory and to let yourself be seen. There's a time for reticence and behind-the-scenes action, and then there's a time for the grand musical production announcing your big ideas with flair and some biodegradable glitter.

7. ***What is waiting to be born with the sun in my life?*** The Moon is remote, representative of anything, everything, the impossible hanging right there in the sky almost every night, as if just waiting for us to reach out and grab it. What's waiting to be born to us in the days to come is the moon, the unknown, the mysterious reflected reality of all our hopes and dreams.

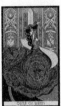

Blue Moon

Keywords
Opportunities, chance, the Joker, the wild card

*B*lue moons are wild-card events that happen in different months and different seasons every few years, although recently there were two pretty close together in one year, but that won't happen again until well into the 2030s. When we say that something only happens "once in a blue moon," we mean it's something that only happens rarely, and those of us of the woo persuasion find magic in the rare astrological happening. It's the perfect time for special workings and spells that don't fit into an everyday practice; it's time to bust out the big plans, think big, and believe big. I used to believe that blue moons were actually blue and that that's why they were rare. But then one day I sort of shook myself awake and realized that that made no sense whatsoever from a scientific perspective, no matter how perfectly it made sense poetically, and since the world seems to be run these days from a scientific perspective, there must be a better definition of what a blue moon actually is. As with so many other things, the internet (specifically TimeAndDate.com, in this case) came to the rescue:

> "There are two different definitions for a Blue Moon. A seasonal Blue Moon is the third Full Moon of an astronomical season that has four Full Moons. A monthly Blue Moon is the second Full Moon in a calendar month with two Full Moons."

Thanks, internet! But other than that it's rare, what does it mean? It made me think about how arbitrary our calendar system is, that it doesn't take enough of the sweep of the moon and stars into account to satisfy my poetic soul. But then again, if I was in charge of the calendars, every day would be two days long, so maybe it's better that they didn't ask me.

If you think about the Fool in the Tarot, it's a wild card. The Fool in the first Tarot decks, centuries ago, didn't have a number and was used (and played) as a wild card. The Fool in the Rider-Waite-Smith Tarot deck has the number zero, and as such can be inserted into the Major Arcana flow anywhere. It can represent the tabula rasa we all are at the beginning of our life's journey— or the one who has achieved enlightenment at the end of a lifetime of experiences. Blue moons are wild cards too: extras, add-ins that still have a demonstrable effect on the state of play in their realm of influence. Blue moons can change things. They shake things up, move things around, and start and complete things in ways no one can see coming. They help a player win her game or lead her to overplay her hand. They promise everything and nothing and, as such, are the ultimate Trickster, the chaos agent reveling in the existence of all possibilities before decisions begin to melt them away.

Questions to Ponder

Consider the following as you shuffle your deck. Where do we need a fresh start right now? If we were going to ask for a deus ex machina to fix our life story, or a getaway time machine, or a new journey or plan, what would it be? If the sky is the limit, how high is our sky? How can the energy of this blue moon be harnessed and drawn upon to bring luck and change into our lives? What is our wild card, our talisman of hope and fortune for better luck and brighter days when the light of the blue moon passes? How can the seasonal energies be tapped into to assist in the work? Is it spring when this blue moon appears, or summer? Is it a seasonal blue moon (the third of four in a season) or a monthly blue moon? Can we use that information to more specifically direct our prayers?

Southern Hemisphere

The timing of the blue moons may be a little different due to local time differences, but this extra wild-card moon will appear wherever on earth you live, and its implications will be the same.

Spread

After shuffling, draw four cards and lay them out according to the following diagram.

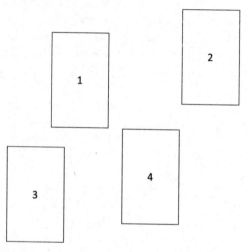

Positions

1. ***What is my wild card right now?*** What do I have up my sleeve that nobody knows about except me? What's my secret magic, my trick, my special sauce that can change everything? We might already have an idea about what this is, but even if we're a practiced magician with loads of rabbits in our hat, there still might be something new and unknown that needs to be revealed in our life right now.

2. ***How can I best play my wild card right now?*** Should I play it or hold it? Is the time right, or should I wait a bit

longer? I'm not much of a poker player, so having this sort of advice is useful for me. I need tips and instructions for making the best use of my secret magic.

3. ***Where in my life do I need to take a leap of faith?*** This is another question whose answer could be pretty obvious (or not) depending on where we are in our lives and what things look like. But if it's not obvious, some guidance on where to leap could be helpful. Where do I need new hope and new experiences? Where should I be looking?

4. ***What is the Fool's little dog trying to tell me?*** In many Tarot decks, the Fool is accompanied by an animal companion, often a white dog. In the Divine Deco Tarot, the Fool's dog dances behind him, perhaps waiting to see if the Fool will fall off the cliff he's moving toward, or if once he steps off he will land. Is the dog warning the Fool about the cliff he is about to step off of? Or is the dog perhaps excited about the new adventure he is embarking on with the Fool? What message is he trying to convey?

Sample Reading

Our blue moon sample spread shows us each of the suits except the Pentacles, and even the Temperance angel in the spread's one Major Arcana card is ankle-deep in the emotional waters of the heart. For this particular reading, at least, it seems like we'll be working with the heart's voice and leaving the earthy material world alone for a bit.

1. ***What is my wild card right now?*** The 3 of Swords may seem like a sad wild card to have, but think about it. Our sensitivity and empathy are our superpowers! We're able to feel the world's sorrow and grief, but that means we can also feel its joy and delight, its contentment, its peace.

2. ***How can I best play my wild card right now?*** The 4 of Wands reinforces the need for boundaries and shows us home, family, connections, and the people and relationships that are most important to us. Maybe the 4 of Wands refers to the home of our heart, the space where we hold our most precious ideas and plans. If so, holding compassion for ourselves as we learn to bring those plans out into the light seems like a reasonable and good idea.

3. ***Where in my life do I need to take a leap of faith?*** The 7 of Cups shows us what our leap of faith is in life right now, and it's a doozy. It's like asking the universe a yes/no question and getting the answer "mailbox." There are lots of confusing choices in front of us, and whatever we choose is what we choose. That's the leap. We won't know if we made the right choice until after we've hit the ground, and maybe not even then.

4. ***What is the Fool's little dog trying to tell me?*** Temperance can mean multiple things: balance, prudence, walking the middle path between extremes, and creating new things out of disparate ingredients that no one thought of putting together before. The angel of Temperance is an alchemist, among other things, and is telling us that the road forward requires creativity, balance, keeping an even keel, and staying fearlessly on the path.

Conclusion

We've reached the end of the calendar year and have ridden its waves up and down together. If you've been able to work your way through a whole year of Tarot spreads as laid out in this book, or even if you've only used one, it is my fervent wish that it has been useful for you and added some divination magic to your life. Working with the Tarot isn't always easy, but as with any other tool since human beings first began to sharpen rocks and dig with sticks, the more you use it the more familiar you become with it. Maybe using the Tarot even becomes easier over time, but I think it's just a matter of achieving greater levels of confidence as you move on in your journey.

There are so many ways to perceive the world and its wonders, and the Tarot provides us with the ability to deepen our perception. Using it in alignment with the shifting energies of our magical world, as we do when we read the cards during a full or dark moon or on any of the major festivals, might help us to come into closer contact with our nature, our ancestors, our guardian spirits, or even the gods themselves. That's my hope for myself: that using the Tarot will help me learn and understand from those divine sources the way to move forward as a better human being. And that's my hope for everyone else who uses the Tarot as well.

Resources

The following items have been essential to me in learning about and working with the Tarot over the years. They may be helpful to you too.

Books

Tarot for Your Self: A Workbook for the Inward Journey by Mary K. Greer

Seventy-Eight Degrees of Wisdom: A Tarot Journey to Self-Awareness by Rachel Pollack

The Sacred Tarot Unveiled by Allyson Walsh

Decks

The Intuitive Tarot by Cilla Conway

Thoth Tarot by Aleister Crowley

The Rider-Waite-Smith Tarot by Arthur Waite

The Mary-El Tarot by Marie White

Stores and Groups

Ancient Ways in Oakland, California: ancientways.com

East West Bookshop in Mountain View, California: eastwestbooks.org

Northwest Tarot Symposium (NWTS): nwtarotsymposium.com

Tarot History (public Facebook group): facebook.com/groups/1457073457838971

Tarot Media Company: tarotmediacompany.com

Websites

If you want to learn more about Irish pagan spirituality, you can find the Irish Pagan School at irishpagan.school. There is also a YouTube channel connected to the school at youtube.com/@IrishPaganSchool.

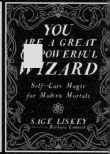

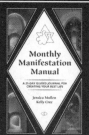

GET THE DECK!

DIVINE DECO
TAROT

GERTA OPARAKU EGY